I0429160

ISLAMIC TERROR

Mr. Mohamed FANDI

To my idols!

ISLAMIC TERROR

Thanks

Without the encouragement of my beloved wife, curiosity and her incontestable support, this book would never see the light. Thank you Rosa M.

Without the smile of my precious daughter, that keeps me going, and the persistent innocent questions of a 7 years-old, this book won't be a reality. Thank you Leyla H.

To my parents, who are Muslims and still don't know I wrote this book: Thank you for being always there for me, I love you. Thank you mom (Zahra), thank you dad (Driss).

To my two brothers Yassine and Amine, thank you for all the support and affection. You are my best pals ever.

Also a very special thanks to my friend Willie G. for all his encouragement.

Without the hours with my dog "Fibi" sitting next to me while writing this book, I won't be able to find the joy to be distracted from all the horrific events in this essay. Thanks Fibi.

Preface

Prevent and save lives. The main goal for writing this book is to find a solution to the Islamic Terrorist attacks, and try to stop them from happening. It's an essay to keep track on the movements and know when such attacks could happen, and therefore be able to prevent them. It is a book trying to find solutions and prevent future attacks to occur. This book is a way to understand the events throughout history so we can prevent them from happening. How the pattern, of such attacks, goes on is one of the most important questions to study. It is a work dedicated to understand the mind of terrorist and what's next, on his or her agenda. There should be a solution to stop Islamic Terrorist attack, and this book could get close to such conclusion. For the well-being of humans and Muslims themselves, a halt and definite stop to such attacks should be a priority to be addressed. This book is a close answer to many understanding related to how wrong the attacks on freedom, attacks on humans, attacks on the right to live and cohabitate... there is no justification of such Islamic Terrorist attacks; they are just not right, and should be abolished and extinct. This essay, book, is a try to understand why such Islamic Terrorist attacks happen, how, when and how can we stop them from happening. Once the pattern is understandable, it would be easier to catch the attacks before they happen. It's also a try to critique all parts responsible for such hatred, killing and corruption throughout the world, especially the Muslim world. Responsibilities are to be shared mostly between fanatic Muslims from all walk of life. Kings and presidents of most Muslim countries are the number one responsible for spreading hatred through the abuse of religious power to their benefits. Moroccan's King is an example of how passive actions could lead to the growth of Terrorism in such country, and other neighbor countries. He has to step down from his throne, as any other corrupted responsible that has done nothing to stop the cancer of Jihad Terrorism. He, as any other Arab leader, is corrupted by the need to satisfy all, and only, his needs. He used the religious power to keep his throne untouchable in depend of his own people's miserable lives, willing to slaughter anybody that contradicted his ideas. He is using a religious' title; calling himself as Emir of Muslims (Mouminins), as a spiritual leader that can't be touched, because of his religious immunity. How in the world can we allow a person to be our god in earth!!! We should be born as free men, not having to be owned by a King, one that never respected people's freedom to democracy, and religion choice. During the month of Ramadan, you will be prosecuted by a crime if somebody sees you eating in the street, you will be taken to jail if a police officer sees you with a sandwich in your hand or a can of soda. Authorities have the right to arrest you if you are an Arab eating during the day in Ramadan. It is shameless not to have the right to do what you please, as far as you respect other people around you.

The king of Morocco is one example of how hypocrisy can still be tolerated in many Arab and Muslim countries. He is a disgrace for this North African country. No progress whatsoever has been seen during his reign, or his father's.

World´s geography.

Geography and politics are hugely predominant factors and important areas in diverse ways to understand all the conflicts related to human behavior. It is an international behavior related to the geographic placement of every person and country. It explain and predict at the same time any international political behavior throughout the geographical variable situation of every country and entity.

Every country, and therefore individual, is destined to have a lifestyle determined by its geographic location in the world. It is a placement that cannot be changed under any circumstances.

Westerns countries have the privilege to be located in places with sufficient resources. However, countries located in Africa, for example, have the bad luck to be placed in areas with very limited resources.

With globalization, the world have seen individuals move from one place to another in an easier way than 100 years ago. They can leave their home countries and live in other places if conditions were somehow too inconvenient or hard for them.

It is also a necessity to understand, that every behavior is related to the resources each country or entity has to offer. A person would be looking for a better life if the resources the country he lives in doesn't provide, so the flux to emigrate and leave everything behind is a necessity. Geography is, by definition, a dead end. It is the only reality that can't be changed. Governments and states have the obligation to survive in a peaceful manner to such reality. Once they fail to cohabitate, then emerge problems and clashes of nations.

The placement of each country and civilization have guided the world to a more elaborated and complex at the same time of each race and religion. The people tend to feel more secure with people from the same color or race, or just religion. Every country is destined and obliged to live in harmony with their neighbor country. In case cohabitation doesn't occur, which happen in most of the cases, it's hard to find peace. Europe have the advantage to forge two main concept, color and religion. Most of the European countries have been living in harmony due to their unified skin color (white) and unified religion (Christianity). They get their strength by all the diversity that Africa and Asia are known for, as diverse continents. The economic difficulties that Africa or even South America endure give more opportunities to Europe or North America to get more powerful.

Geography is a very important and a main factor for the development of any society. Every group depend closely of how the others do.

Few centuries ago, Egyptians or Romans ruled the world. Their geographic location helped in their developments. To compete economically, the world was limited to Europe, part of Asia and part of Africa. Nowadays, the United States of America is the main powerful economy. With globalization, it is really hard to do better than USA. All the world have the opportunity to show their strength. As a conclusion, it is impossible to top such society.

The world have to accept the geographic repartition of wealth and compete in an economic market dominated and controlled by the most powerful country in the world; USA.

Nostalgia on how the Arabs or Muslim civilization ruled the world centuries ago create some kind of regret and hatred for some fanatics. Some terrorist leaders and groups use this concept to grow more and more hatred toward the west countries (European and American society). Those groups use religion as the main weapon. They use Islam as the only way out for their daily problems. Taking lives, most of the time innocent lives, is not the solution. However, they find joy and revenge to what "have been taking from them". Instead of competing in a civilized way to get their societies better, they chose the easy way, which is carrying out with their terrorist acts.

Geography has been playing a major act on slowing down the Islamic Terrorist acts. But, at the same time, also made it a necessity for the Terrorists and radicalized Muslim leaders to justify their violent acts. Such Terrorist groups keep on killing civilians anywhere they could. Geography had helped them getting stronger in some places like Africa. For example Nigeria or Libya have developed a strong Islamic radicalization because of the proximity that situated them close to Muslim dominated populated areas. If the borders between races and societies didn't exist, hatred between religions wouldn't exist.

In the western countries, the presence of terrorist individuals or group is very limited. However, because of the new technology, internet or other ways of communications, some terrorist groups or leaders have been in contact with people living in those countries and try every day to radicalize them or join their groups. To get more support from their own people, such terrorist groups find themselves obliged to recruit people living in western countries. Islamic Terrorist leaders are trying to globalize their concept to become more and more worldwide phenomena.

They are using geography as a new concept to be more present in other countries. The more countries in which Terrorists execute their barbaric' acts, the more "field" they "think" are claiming. They consider themselves winning more lands. Such tactics make the Islamic Terrorist groups build a strong propaganda within their own community. An example of such tactics have been used by Al-Qaeda ex-leader, Usama ben Laden, after the New York attacks, showing him enjoying the attacks. He later took his 9/11 attacks as a win over the western way of life. He have proven to other Terrorist groups that what he did was a "win". It would have never been a win for him if it was not for the geographic locations of the targets. His main goal was to export the Jihad to the western world.

The future of each country and its struggle with terrorism depend mostly with the geographic location of each society.

World´s history of Terrorism.

Globalization is a very fresh, new and still in the making phenomena in our society. The world's history has been shaped more locally than internationally. We are in the 21st century, and it took us more than 20 centuries to elaborate a way of living within a single society. With the globalization and the world becoming like a small village, it is still too early to establish a peaceful world wide atmosphere to live in a harmony. It will happen but not in a short time. The world has to establish a wide range of laws that govern the society as a whole not as a single entity. In order to live in a peaceful world with secure non-conflictual history diversity has to expand limitlessly.

The world has gone from solving local problems and issues, to be confronted to an unlimited international and inter-socio problems.

Islamic countries have not been part of Western developments in the last few centuries. With such transition, and being considered behind in time, technology and economy, the Arab and Islam world wanted to get involved in such change. However, it can be done with radicalism, because nothing can be accepted with force.

However, Islamic extremism goes back to the 7th century to the Kharijites. They were a Muslim group that differ themselves from Sunni and Shi'a Muslims. They declared other Muslims to be unbelievers, therefore infidels and deemed to be worthy of death. It's a radical doctrine placing anybody who doesn't follow the exact interpretation of Islam as not worthy to live, an approach to Takfir.

The history of terrorism is a history of well-known and historically significant individuals, entities and incidents associated, whether rightly or wrongly, with terrorism. The roots and practice of terrorism can be traced at least to the 1st-century. During the 1st century CE, the Jewish Zealots in Judaea Province rebelled, killing prominent collaborators with Roman rule. In 6 CE, according to contemporary historian Josephus, Judas of Galilee formed a small and more extreme offshoot of Zealots, the Sicarii (dagger men). Their efforts were also directed against Jewish "collaborators", including temple priests, Sadducees, Herodians, and other wealthy elites. According to Josephus, the Sicarii would hide short daggers under their cloaks, mingle with crowds at large festivals, murder their victims, and then disappear into the panicked crowds. Their most successful assassination was of the high priest Jonathan.

In the late 11th century, the Hashshashin (the Assassins) arose, an offshoot of the Isma'ili sect of Shia Muslims. Led by Hassan-i-Sabbah (the first Islamic Terrorist) and opposed to Fatimid rule, the hashshashin militia seized Alamut and other fortress strongholds across Persia. They were known by killing city governors and military commanders. In order to create alliance with militarily powerful neighbors, they were conducting their operations against notorious and known figures in the high governance scale. Because of their small numbers, they couldn't fight local military. Such acts have been used to intimidate political enemies or inspire revolts.

From 1793 till 1794, France have seen the Terror or the Reign of terror was a period of eleven months during the French Revolution when the ruling Jacobins employed violence, including mass executions by guillotine, in order to intimidate the regime's enemies and compel obedience to the state. They killed more than 40,000 and among the guillotined were Louis XVI and Marie Antoinette. The Jacobins, most famously Robespierre, sometimes referred to themselves as "terrorists," and the word originated at that time.

In the 19th century, powerful, stable, and affordable explosives were developed, global integration reached unprecedented levels and often radical political movements became widely influential. The use of dynamite has been helpful to their strategies. All over Europe, acts of terrorists have been spread out throughout Ireland, Russia, France or Spain. Individual Europeans also engaged in politicaly motivated violence. For example, in 1893, Auguste Vaillant, a French anarchist, threw a bomb in the French Chamber of Deputies in which one (1) person was injured.

The United States of America have also seen terrorist movements before this century. After the Civil War, on 1865, six Confederate veterans created the Ku Klux Klan (KKK). The organization had 550,000 men. Its political ideology was built around many principles as White Supremacy, white Nationalism, Nativism, Anti-immigration, Anti-communism, Christian Terrorism, Anti-Catholicism, Antisemitism, Homophobism, and Neo-fascism. They used violence, murder and acts of intimidation such cross burning to oppress in particular African Americans, and created a sensation with its masked forays' dramatic nature.

The Ottoman Empire also suffered many acts of violence against its reign. In apparent decline, few nationalist groups (one of whom were Armenian Federation) used terrorism against the Ottoman Empire. By its terrorist acts, the militants were trying to bring in a European intervention that would force the Ottoman Empire to surrender control of its Armenian territories. On august, 1896, a Sunni militant led 26 members in capturing the Imperial Ottoman Bank in Constantinople. They demanded European intervention to stop the Hamidian massacres and the creation of an Armenian state.

In the 20th century, revolutionary nationalism continued to motivate political violence, much of it directed against western colonial powers. The Irish Republican Army campaigned against the British in the 1910s and inspired the Zionist groups of Hagannah, Irgun and Lehi to fight the British throughout the 1930s in the Palestine mandate. And Like IRA and the Zionist groups, the Muslim Brotherhood used bombings and assassinations to try to free Egypt from British control. ETA, an acronym for Euskadi Ta Askatasuna, was also an armed Basque nationalist and separatist group in northern Spain and southwestern France. Active form 1959 till 2011, ETA has been held responsible for killing 829 people and injuring thousands. It is described as a terrorist group by Spain, the United Kingdom, France, the United States, and the European Union.

Centuries ago, Islam ruled a large part of the world. They were very developed. They invaded some parts of Europe. However, after the beginning of the 20th century, the glory of Islam were over. Instead of getting up and forging a better economy and values, they just start the blaming game. Blaming the western culture, the Jews and Christians for its fall doesn't make it any better for them. Some militants and terrorist groups still believe in the supremacy of Muslims. While they can't beat them economically they try to kill them. It is being an act of being cowards. Some leaders, like Kaddafi's Libya, Khomeini's Iran, or even Saudi-Arabia's royal family supported and funded terrorists around the world.

Radical Islam have only one goal: to make Islam the only religion. Their supporters live in a dream land. It appears the only way to do so is to strap a bomb around their waist. What a ridiculous way of wasting lives.

The history can, and must change. Our path can only change to better or worse. And that is the purpose of life. Terror can't and won't last forever. If there is one thing humanity learnt from history is that, the way life is and the lessons of history taught us that good things prevail always. By nature, and humanity destiny, the way things tend to develop is in a positive and constructive way, not destructive. Terrorism, throughout history, did never win.

Wars throughout history have proven the implication of governments and political parties to benefit from them.

The passivity and implication of states, governments, presidents and royal families to the raise of terrorism have not been demonstrated directly. However, many Middle East and North African presidents and kings have been taking prides and money to promote Terrorism indirectly.

Somebody is benefiting from it, and that is why it is still happening.

Danger of any Religion. Press and media's rule, and its impact on Terrorism.

Every day, at various western airports there are still calls for people to go and attend chapel. Anybody can assist to such religious' brainwash or "manipulation". It's basically close and similar to what Muslims do five times a day. The presence of churches or mosques have been a negligible point and not controllable one.

Sometimes, technology and press involvement go in a way to help spread the problem, indirectly, while making terrorists notoriously known and famous.

We should not only mention attacks in which people died or injured but also praise those failed terrorist attempts due to the courage and hard work of people to stop them from happening. Those failed attempts save more humans lives than the one that happened. They should have more media coverage than the ones that happened.

False information is also perceived as a major factor to such propaganda for or against religions. It's easy to make people follow an idea. Such idea can be bad or good. It is very rare when ideas are spread to make a better life for people. It is usually the other way, when politicians use propaganda to gain power. All the Terrorist attacks have some political or economic gain for some group of people. Most of the time, such people try to gain political power, and therefore gain elections or money by having people following their actions (by blowing themselves up). Anybody who claim to die for a religious cause is a selfish person. The ones who ordered them to do so, example Osama Ben Laden, or ISIL's leader, are just dictators, and don't accept any ideas or ideology different than theirs. They use the factor of hatred to fuel their followers and make them commit suicide bombs.

Why so much hatred involved? They use the economy as a major factor to influence them. The economy is so bad in the third world countries, where Terrorist Bombers can give their lives with nothing in exchange, they blew themselves up in a second. Leaders in Terrorist Islamic groups can change a person from being a good citizen to a Terrorist in few weeks, or days, or sometimes months. Internet and technology make things even worse when people in third world ¨see how westerners live¨.

The media can very manipulative, and only give the information that make a big sale for them. They are controlled by governments and people desire. No media would publish anything that doesn't give them any payback. No audience means no media. No readiness to consume a kind of news will result in no-publication. The demand (consumers, or readers of news) must equal the offer (media or news).

Timeline to publish a piece of news is also very important. In some places people don't get the news about something that happened at the same time as other places. Countries are very prudent and manipulatives of their news. The wait to not publish the news as soon as they arrive is to establish the importance and impact of the product toward the population. Governments and department states get involved, therefore, that can lead to false or fraudulent news, or just not important and expired.

The relativity that makes the world live like in a small village has its benefits and disadvantage. People that live in poor countries envy anything in other advanced economic countries. Some Muslims, particularly the ones that hate anything about people with other beliefs still can't get that the world we live in is a world of competition, not only their world. It's a planet that belong to everybody. They just need to accept the order of the world, and try to compete fairly, not by killing innocent people.

It's a human instinct that a person hate on other when they have something the other person doesn't have. With the Internet, people in the Muslim world see how the people in the developed countries, "Christians" or "Caucasian" live and envy them.

Of course, not all the Terrorists are born in poor conditions, some of them come from the same civilized countries, where they grow and got educated. Those people got brain washed by all the internet propaganda and Islamic Supremacy. The Islamist Supremacy is a concept that gives the right only to Muslims as the leaders and everybody else should be slave. It is a wrong concept and racist concept that should be banned by humanity.

Can the world, ever, live in a harmony... we all look different, so...?

Steps should be taken, not drastic ones, but with time and passion. Being positive and accepting everybody's habits and costumes has to be the rule not the exception. Barack Obama, U.S. President, on his last State of the Union speech has mention wisely and positively his support to good and humanity as a whole. That's the example everybody have to follow. Live in harmony, love and peace.

Lot of time should be taking in consideration to educate people on what should be the right concept for a better life, for a coherent coexistence between races, and not hate which is easier to build).

Feel accepted has a big effect on people's mind, they want to be integrated. That's all they seek, and once they don't feel that security and acceptance, they start to rebel, either by avoiding integration witch is the peaceful way or by fighting the other side.

The result of fighting can lead to an extreme act of terrorism trying to exterminate the other side.

A clash of cultures can easily erupt if the media and politics don't minimize the importance of such acts. With their coverage and given importance to such acts, people start hating on other people based on their color or race. Regardless of how anybody act, it is hard for a human being not to judge other races, that don't look or act alike. Globalization has helped those behaviors to be easily spread out.

Nowadays, the world seems like a small village. All movements are coordinated in a smaller, faster way than before. People travel more now than they used to. They can see how the rich live and how the poor lives in each country. Some third world countries still don't accept the reality.

The only exit for them is to kill the western lifestyle, so they can be even with their reality, which is based on hate and using a religious mentality to execute their killings and hatred for western way of living. They became uncontrollable, they became terrorists. Based on their religious beliefs, they are sure they have the absolute right to go ahead with their acts of terrorism, and for them death will be just a next endless step that they accept with pride. Mentally those Muslims, or any other religion terrorists, do their acts based on god's will. They use a non-existence entity to justify their acts. Religion can be a source of happiness or a big source of hatred towards others.

Religion should be between an individual himself or herself and whatever that person believes on, period.

However, if a statement has to be made on whatever god exist or no, the answer is no. Were all these prophets lying is the question we can't find an answer to unless we investigate the dead. We need evidence. We only have stories.

Culture shock is when they born in a place where they are not accepted. Those new born grow up in a separate atmosphere, then they start questioning themselves, why can´t they own the place, they feel it´s not fair not to be accepted as part of any society, they don't have a determinant identity... race is an important visible factor.

The main problem ... is killing, why terrorist kill... for the Muslims terrorists, killing under the act of jihad, it is kind of accomplishment, for them nothing is wrong with it, their deep beliefs dictate to them that it´s a success to do so... well it´s wrong to take another person life for any reason regardless...

How did we get here... to this point... it doesn't make any sense, because of a person beliefs, thoughts, customs, religions or whatsoever, life should be ceased. We should not judge a person because of those believes. Nowadays, we point fingers at people because of their race, because of their color, because of their look, accent, behavior, really... is that the direction we want to take, where that direction is taking us... where is the end of it... we tried it many times, the last time was with Hitler. Resume: with the way the world is today we are destined to coexist, or face unfair treatment or injustice death, due to a person´s color.

Should an extreme idea be eliminated or tolerated? Should a verse in the bible or the Koran be eliminated or just modified for the well-being of humanity?

Tolerance is a temporary factor; that need for the two parties to be at the same level of understanding and education of such problem or phenomena, to succeed and be taking into consideration. There can't be tolerance if one of the two sides doesn't believe in unconditional coexistence. The minimum should start with respecting a person's life to live the way he, or she, wants.

Because of the actual events: attacks in Paris 11/13/2015, New York 9/11/2001, attacks in Spain, England, Bali, Casablanca... etc. there is a necessity to target one point here. If the religion of Islam doesn't give full recognition of other religions it should not be any kind of tolerance and Islam should be banned from earth. It's sad to come to such conclusion, but for the well-being of humanity, Islam need some major modifications.

Enough already. What is the point? What is the purpose, plan or target? If there is one thing those murderers are doing, is, to make the whole world hate, not only Islam as a killing machine, but most importantly Muslims. People are being hated and targeted because of their color, race, beliefs, opinions or just their first or last name.

We can easily live in harmony if all religions respect and recognize the other side's opinion. Opinions related to everything from simple customs to major issues, or just a celebration of any religious or no-religious holiday, such Christmas, Hanukkah, Ramadan or thanksgiving.

An example of how wrong a religion can be: why a person can't eat pork? It is understandable if the reason is a healthy one, but not acceptable just because somebody say it and forbade it. Crispy bacon is delicious. If you eat just small portions and you do some exercise on a routine basics, I don't see why pork is bad and illegal in a spiritual concept. It is something your body will digest then, later, get rid of.

Why does it bother god, if there is one anyway, that a person eat something? Why does it bother a Muslim nation as a whole that a person is eating pork, to the point of forbidding selling it in a market?

The answer is that tradition and habits make rules to reality. It takes time and effort to change a concept.

Well, the western's civilizations and people made a mistake all the way; racism against blacks. People with color have been treated in a bad way and marginalized to a second level citizen. That's what pushed the Islam to a higher position, because they gave them freedom from white supremacy.

When a person has to kill another person, under a religious pretext, it's easier to do so by involving god. Apparently, no other choice. It is only an idea that has been developed to justify such criminal act, that's all. Quietly, nicely and with a plan. It's hard to stop it. But, it's not impossible to prevent it; when God is involved to justify such a horrible, but still forgivable act. It is the magical power of mighty God!!!

A Terrorist is a lazy, unaccomplished person, comparing to someone who succeeded to become an active person in the society. A terrorist doesn't go through lot of practicing, it's an easy lousy job that anybody can do; two weeks of training and you ready; comparing to a sportive person, for instance, who want to make it to the Olympics, it's a hard work; every day training. It's constancy, it's a work that need to be improved, and it's a success. Terrorists can do an attack in a second, no preparation, no studying, nothing; it's as easy as being lazy. Most of the terrorists never went to school, they don't have any degree or dreams, except what they have been teaching them to accomplish; they will get Virgins, after they die!

Events developments from 70s to 80s.

September 23, 1970- Jordan- Terrorist attack carried out by PFLP (party of front liberation of Palestine) and coined "skyjack Sunday". 3 planes (TWA, Swissair, and Pan Am) hijacked en route to the U.S., no casualties with more than 400 hostages, then later the planes were blown, and governments agreed to PFLP's demands, releasing some terrorists from jail and hostages released.

September 5, 1972- Germany- Munich Massacre in Germany by Islamic Black September militants. Few Palestinian Terrorists seize 11 athletes in the Olympic Village in Munich. The toll after the siege was of 9 hostages dead and 5 terrorists killed.

March 1, 1974, Sudan- some diplomats have been taken by Islamic terrorists from Saudi Arabian Embassy in Khartoum, Sudan, two (2) U.S. nationals killed.

January 19, 1975, France- Arab Islamic terrorists attacked Orly International airport, Paris, France, seizing 10 hostages from a bathroom. French authorities provided safe Heaven for the Terrorists giving them a plane to fly them back to safety in Baghdad, Iraq.

History proved how wrong it is to make a deal with terrorists. In the 70s it was seen as nobody's problem to fight any Palestinians hijacking airplanes. It was seen as a right to hijack a plane and ask to release other terrorists. Allowing Palestinians to use any method as a way to fight Israelis have become an excuse for terrorists to use the same weapons later on their quest to kill innocent people in the years and decades to come. As the saying dictate in other words: "you should stop the bleeding the moment it occurs, later might be too late".

November 4, 1979, Iran- Terrorists seized the U.S. Embassy in Tehran and took 66 American diplomats hostage. 13 of them freed, but the remaining 53 were held until their release on January 20, 1981.

November 20 to December 4th, 1979, Saudi Arabia- the Grand Mosque in Mecca seizure occurred when Islamic extremist insurgents calling for the overthrow of the House of Saud took over Masjid al-Haram. 250 dead, 600 wounded, because the insurgents declared that the Mahdi "the redeemer of Islam" has arrived in the form of one of their leaders and called on Muslims to obey him.

During the second half of the 20th century, most of the terrorist Islamic violence occurred in the last 10 to 20 years. It all, mostly, took a starting point of Islamic pure radicalism, at the 1980s, with organized mass or individual Islamic terrorist attacks. Following are the major Islamist terrorist events that took place in the 1980s era.

The 80s:

November 11, 1982- Lebanon. Tyre headquarters bombings: 91 dead, 55 injured. April 18, 1983- the April 1983 U.S. Embassy bombing, in Beirut, Lebanon, 63 dead, 120 injured. October 12, 1983- The 1983 Beirut barracks bombing by the Islamic Jihad Organization: 307 dead, 75 injured. December 12, 1983- 1983 Kuwait bombings; the 90 minute coordinated attack of six key foreign and Kuwaiti installations including embassies, airport and petro-chemical plants; 6 dead. September 20, 1984- the 1984 United States embassy annex bombing in Beirut, Lebanon, 24 dead. April 12, 1985- El Descanso bombing, 18 dead 82 injuries. October 27, 1985- Achille Lauro hijacking, four men representing the Palestine Liberation Front (PLF) hijacked the Italian MS Achille Lauro liner off the coast of Egypt, sailing off the coast from Alexandria to Ashdod, Israel, 1 dead. December 27, 1985- Rome and Vienna airport attacks, 23 dead 139 injured. June 14, 1985- TWA Flight 847, Greece, 1 dead. April 2, 1986- TWA Flight 840 bombing: 4 dead, 7 injured, Greece. September 6, 1986- Neve Shalom Synagogue attack; 22 dead, Turkey. England, December 21, 1988- 1988 Lockerbie bombing, 270 dead. Israel, July 7, 1989- Tel Aviv Jerusalem bus 405 suicide attack, near Kiryat Yearim; 16 dead.

Ten (10) years, from 1980 to end of 1989, there have been a total of 13 attacks related to Islamic Terrorism, with 846 dead, and 478 injured victims.

Then the 90s:

February 4, 1990- a bus in Egypt carrying Israeli tourists was attacked by Islamic Jihad Movement in Palestine, 11 dead and 17 injured. February 2, 1992 Chinese Urumqi bombings, 3 dead and 23 injured. March 17, 1992- Buenos Aires attack on Israeli embassy, 29 dead and 242 injured. The Islamic Jihad Organization, operates under Hezbollah entity, linked to Iran, claimed responsibility for the bombing. January 25, 1993- CIA shootings at its headquarters in Virginia; 2 dead, 3 injured. February 26, 1993- World Trade Center bombing, in New York; 6 dead and 1042 injured. March 12, 1993- various blasts in Mumbai, India; 257 dead. July 2, 1993- Turkey, the incident occurred on a Friday afternoon; thousands of Sunni locals in Sivas (the Turkish city where it happened), after attending Friday prayers in a nearby mosque, marched to a hotel where a conference was taking place and set the building on fire. Attending the conference was a left-wing Turkish intellectual, Aziz Nesin, who translate the Satanic Verses's Salman Rushdie's controversial novel about Mahomet, the personae mastermind who created Islam. The curios part was that, the assault took almost eight hours, with no response or intervention from the police, military or fire department, to stop the attacks. The fire claimed 35 lives. April 6, 1994- Israel, Afula Bus suicide bombing, 8 people dead and 55 injured. One week after, April 13, 1994- Israel, Hadera bus station suicide bombing, 5 dead and 30 injured. July 18, 1994- Argentina, Buenos Aires Jewish Center AMIA bombing, it was Argentina deadliest bombing ever, took 85 lives and 300 injured. Nobody has been hold responsible for the attacks, but blames has been directed to Iran. July 26, 1994- England, London Israeli Embassy attack, 20 wounded. Responsibility was directed to Hezbollah, Iran, and 2 Palestinians, science graduate educated in the UK, were found guilty, they were sentenced to 20 years in jail. October 19, 1994- Israel, the Dizengoff Street bus bombing in Tel Aviv, was a Hamas

(Palestinian Islamic organization) suicide terrorist attack that killed 22 and wounded 50. November 11, 1994- Israel, Netzarim Junction bicycle bombing, 3 dead and 12 injured, claimed by Palestine's Islamic Jihad Organization; after the attack, Palestinian police arrested 100 Islamic militants, and raided a mosque.

Governments and authorities are to be blamed also for allowing those groups to exist and operate. Police didn't intervene in the 1993 Turkish attack, 1994 in Argentina, police didn't arrest any individuals, same year Yasser Arafat, Palestine Liberation Organization Chairman, condemned the bicycle attack bombing and made raids on houses and a mosque... the whole world knew and the leaders never stepped up to stop this scandal. Why?

December 24, 1994- Algeria, Air France Flight hijacked in Algiers by three members of Armed Islamic Group of Algeria and another terrorist. 7 dead including 4 hijackers and 25 injured. January 22, 1995- Israel, the Beit Lid suicide bombing claimed by Palestinian Islamic Jihad; 20 killed and 69 injured. January 30, 1995- Algeria, a car bomb outside of a police station, 42 dead, and 286 wounded. July 20, 1995- India, a bomb on a motor scooter exploded at a marketplace in Jammu. A Pakistani extremist Organization called Harkat-ul-Mujahideen, claimed the attack, 17 dead and 100 wounded. This organization has been designated a terrorist organization by the United Nations, the United Kingdom and the United States. However, in 2012, the Pakistani Government didn't list this group in the list of banned organizations.

Again, governments and local authorities failing to participate actively in banishing such terrorist organizations. Two more examples here: one of Algeria and the other of Pakistan, even helping terrorist entities, or juts closing their eyes and letting such evil prevail. The Algerian government, via its secret service's colonels was helping with the killing and execution. In two bombs Paris, France, in the summer of 1995, the operation was (allegedly) run by Colonel Souames Mahmoud, head of the secret service at the Algerian embassy in Paris. Therefore, it seems like the Algerian government was involved in atrocities and attacks, contradicting what the Government was claiming in public.

July 24, 1995, Israel- Ramat Gan bus bombing claimed by Hamas, 6 dead and 33 injured. Why Hamas isn't recognized as a terrorist organization by Russia, Norway, Switzerland, Brazil, Turkey and China? It's understandable that it is not recognized by Iran or Qatar to be such terrorist organization!!! Hamas is designated as a terrorist organization by the European Union, Israel, Canada, Egypt, Japan and the United States. The world must act unified if we want to demolish such entities. However, countries like Russia, a big powerful state, have to change their approach toward supporting regimes and organizations that kills innocent people, or give supports to extreme ideologies, such Islamic jihadist.

From July 25 to October 17, 1995, France- Paris Metro and RER bombings, a series of bombs and killings took place in Paris, resulting on 8 deaths and 157 non-fatal injuries, the Armed Islamic Group took responsibility. This was an exportation or extension to the Algerian Civil War in France. October 20, 1995, Croatia- suicide bombing, kills one; the assailant, and 29 injured. February 25 & March 3, 1996, Israel- 45 killed and 52 injured in the Jaffa Road bus bombing. March 4, 2996, Israel- Hamas attacked again, 13 killed and 130 injured the Dizengoff Center suicide bombing, a Jewish holiday of Purim. April 18, 1996, Egypt- 18 dead and 17 injured in an Islamic gunmen fire on the Europe hotel in Cairo. June 20, 1996, Saudi Arabia, Khobar Towers Bombing, 19 marines from the causalities among 20 dead, the goal of terrorists was to get the U.S. military to leave the country, they didn't and the result was 20 killed and 372 injured. February 25, 1997, China- three bombs exploded in Xinjiang, china, 9 dead including 3 children, injuries 74. March 21, 1997, Israel- Hamas, the Palestinian extremist authority attacking by a suicide bomber a Tel Aviv sidewalk café, killing 3 wounding 46. July 30, 1997, Israel- The 1997 Mahane Yehuda Market bombings killing again 16 and injuring 178, carried out by Hamas. September 18, 1997, Bosnia and Herzegovina, targeting Croatian civilians and injuring 120 apartments as well as 120 vehicles, it remains the most serious terrorist attack in post-war Bosnia and Herzegovina. A car bombing that injured 29 people. November 17, 1997, Egypt- Luxor massacre, 62 killed and 26 wounded from tourists, due to attacks from Egyptian Islamists, an Egyptian Islamist, Al-Gama'a al-Islamiya, using automatic firearms and knives. February 14, 1998, India- Valentine's day, right? 58 dead and 200 wounded in 12 bomb attacks in different places, 11 locations in the city of Coimbatore, Tamil Nadu, India; extremist terrorism. August 7, 1998, Tanzania- 1998 United States embassy bombings in Tanzania and Kenya. 224 dead and more than 4000 wounded. At last, something good occurs; Osama Bin Laden, for the first time was placed on the FBI ten most-wanted fugitives list. At last, thanks.

That was a logical result of the world's events, starting from more than 50 years ago; by the invasion of Palestine by Israel. An attack has been the fuel of all hatred that been targeted toward all the rest of nations by the end of the 20th century.

As a result, a response by an Islamic entity was a necessity and a normal consequence. It was a result of many years of a negligence by western countries to their demands. Of course, the governments in such miserable Islamic countries have done nothing to prevent such spread of hatred. They can't do nothing because of the way their laws have been linked to religion, a religion of Islam which hate western ideas.

Therefore, it was most likely a possibility to attack any western country or even their own land with terrorist attacks, justified by an ignorant idea, called Jihad.

Surprisingly, by the end of 20th century, nobody in the western countries, except few, knew the hatred placed toward them by Islamic fanatics. Not only, they didn't expect so much hatred, but actually, they trusted, welcome them to live and even grow with them. Why? Because western ideas of humans is way different than Muslims. Westerns, so far (because things can change), have the patient to forgive and respect other religions, regardless of the harm Muslims have done to humanity.

It became a global way of perceiving a Muslim as a terrorist.

He, or she, is a person who doesn't want any other human that doesn't believe in Allah, to exist. By definition, he, or she, is a terrorist. It is a conclusion, and a result of many years of terrorism; hatred, and no respect to other people beliefs. People got killed, murdered, kidnaped and prosecuted. All this has been happening under one "false" justification and one non-sense reason: why a person doesn't believe that Mahomet is the prophet and Allah is the one and only god? Those terrorists kill innocent people because they don't believe in such concept.

Two hundreds (200) years from now, people will be laughing at such "religion" called Islam. It doesn't make any sense, none whatsoever.

Results for the 90s: 1077 dead. 7617 wounded. More than 31 attacks related to Islamic Terrorism.

The 2000s:

April 23- September 19, 2000, Malaysia- kidnapping and hostage crisis, no dead, several injuries, 21 in total after a hostage situation that lasted months. October 12, 2000, Yemen- suicide attack, 17 American sailors were killed and 39 injured; a terrorist attack by Al-Qaeda to a USS Cole. December 22- 2000, India- Red Fort; an attack in Delhi by a Pakistani terrorist group Lashkar-e-Toiba. Location is a significant iconic site in India. Three Indian soldiers lost their lives as a result of the attack. December 24, 2000, Indonesia- churches in Jakarta and seven other Indonesian cities has been bombarded on Christmas Eve. Causalities, 18 killed and 22 injured. Al Qaeda and Jemaah Islamiyah took responsibilities for the series of explosions, more than 18 bombs, took the Indonesian soil.

During the whole year 2000, there have been 4 Islamic terrorist attacks, 38 killed and around 60 people injured.

March 4- 2001, Israel- city of Netanya bombing; killing 3 civilians, ages 58, 70 and 85 years old!!! And injuring more than 60 people. Palestinian Islamic militant group, Hamas, claimed responsibility for the attack. Palestine, didn't agree to arrest people responsible for the attack. Another example of governments helping the spread of such inhuman radicalization, and hatred. April 14- 2001, Bangladesh- a series of bomb attacks, by Harkat-ul-Jihad al-Islami, claimed the lives of 10 people, plus 50 wounded. It happened on the 14th of April, Bengali New Year first day. May 18, 2001, Israel- another bombing in Netanya, killing 5 and injuring more than 100 people. HaSharon mall suicide bombing was an attack claimed by Hamas, the Palestinian Islamist militant. Following the attack Israeli fighter jets attacked Palestinian security forces headquarters in the West bank. May 27, 2001, Philippines- location, Dos Palmas resort, Honda bay. A hostage crisis, where, an Islamic group led by members of Abu Sayyaf seize at least 100 hostages, killed more than 40 and injured more than 60 in over a year, ended on June 7, 2002. June 1- 2001, Israel. An Israeli discotheque has been bombed by a Hamas terrorist, blowing himself up outside of a nightclub in Tel Aviv, Israel. 25 dead and more than 100 casualties. Most the victims were just teenagers, some of them from families emigrated from the former Soviet Union. August 9- 2001, Israel- Sbarro restaurant attack by Hamas, in the Israeli soil, Jerusalem. 15 killed and 130 injured on this terrorist attack on a pizzeria in downtown. September 9- 2001, Israel- a suicide bombing at a train Railway Station in Naharia, Israel, by Arab-Israeli who was sent by Hamas, detonated himself on the crowded platform. 3 dead and 94 wounded.

September 11- 2001, United States of America- 2977 killed and plus 6000 countless wounded. 4 planes hijacked by 19 al-Qaeda members, three hit 3 buildings and one fall from the sky killing everybody on it. Two planes hit the world trade centers in New York, and one hit the Pentagon, Virginia, the fourth plane was supposed to crash into the white house or U.S. Capitol, failed on its way and fall in Pennsylvania.

October 1- 2001, India- 4 bombings on Jammu and Kashmir legislative assembly, 48 deaths, by militants belonging to Jaish-e-Mohammed; group located in Pakistan where they have training camps. November 29- 2001, Israel- Pardes Hanna bus bombing. The bus, travelling through the town of Pardes Hanna-Karhur, en route from Nazareth to Tel Aviv. 3 deaths, 9 injured. Two Palestinian groups took responsibilities of the bombing; Fattah's Al-Aqsa Bridges and Palestinian Islamist militant organization Islamic Jihad. December 2- 2001, Israel- The Palestinian Islamist militant organization Hamas took responsibility of the bombing of a bus in Haifa, killing 15 Israeli civilians and injuring other 40 Israeli subjects. December 13- 2001, India- suicide attack on Indian parliament in New Delhi by Pakistani Islamist terrorist organizations Jaish-E-Mohammad and Lashkar-e-Toiba. Shooting was aimer with the target of creating chaos in the Indian neighbor country and to increase tensions between India and Pakistan. 14 dead and 18 injured, which result to 2001-2002 India-Pakistan standoff.

Year 2001 had witnessed one of the most devastating Islamic terrorist attack in the history of mankind; 9/11/2001 in the United States of America. There have been 12 Islamic terrorist attacks during the whole year, with more than 3137 deaths, and 6543 injured, most of them from September 11, 2001 with 2977 victims killed, and more than 6000 injuries in one single attack.

January 22- 2002, India- Attack on West Bengal, on the American cultural center in Kolkata. Four police and private guard were killed; 5 dead and 20 wounded. An Islamist refused to stop at a checkpoint by the center and started shooting at police guards from an AK-47 assault rifle. Two groups claimed responsibilities, Harkat-ul-Jihad al-Islami and Asif Raza Commandos, which both have ties to radical Islamic groups. Attacks were justified to be protest against "the evil empire of America" quoted by Farhan Malik member of Harkat-ul-Jihad al-Islami.

Israel: January 25 Tel Aviv, January 27 Jerusalem, March 2 Jerusalem, March 9 Jerusalem, March 20 Umm al-Fahm north Israel, March 21 Jerusalem, March 27 Netanya then March 29 also Jerusalem, 2002- were all eight terrorists attacks by Islamic fundamentalists. The first one injured 24 civilians and killed the number, a Palestinian recruited by the Islamic jihad. The second claimed one 1 Israeli civilian life, plus one 1 female bomber, and more than 100 civilians injured. A Palestinian suicide bomber, 28 year old. Al-Aqsa Martyrs Brigade claimed responsibility. The thirst attack took 11 lives plus 1 Palestinian suicide bomber, also claimed by Al-Aqsa Martyrs brigade, a Palestinian terrorist organization. March 9th seen another attack, the fourth this year on the Israeli soil, took 11 Israeli civilians lives and injured more than 54 other Israelis, Hamas claimed responsibility. Bombing occurred in a coffee shop, Café Moment, in downtown Jerusalem, Israel. Next attack was a suicide bombing on a bus, 7 Israelis dead, 27 civilians injured and the Palestinian bomber who exploded himself to death. Islamic Jihad was behind the attack. Al-Aqsa Martyrs Brigades claimed responsibility for the next suicide bombing, which killed 3, plus the Palestinian bomber and at least 42 people injured. The Passover was a massacre suicide bombing, carried by Hamas, at the Park Hotel in Netnya, 30 dead and 140 wounded. One 16 years old Palestinian female bombed herself up at the Shufersal supermarket, Kiryat haYovel neighborhood in Jerusalem, killing 2 Israelis civilians and injured 28 others. Hamas claimed responsibility for the attack.

Attacks can be seen, viewed or explained by different concepts. In the Arab and Muslim countries such attacks are explained by, either the non-forgiveness to the occupation of the Palestine territory, or even more justifying view, a religious necessity to avenge Islam and kill Jews. Feelings of confusion and appurtenance to such ideology just by being a Muslim have been mixed between the two sentiments, and therefore, more and more Muslims integrate such idea. What has been a fight for territory over Palestine occupation by Israel has become more and more a religious conflict.

During the 70s, 80, 90 and even late 2010, the media in the Arab and Muslim world, have never pictured such attacks as terrorist Islamic attack. They have been presented as Palestinians asking for their right to live. Palestine was pictured as a victim in every house in those Arab countries. As a result, kids grew up with the feeling for vengeance to their religion, against Israel.

So when a person place Islam and the rest of religious, you will find a big gap between both sides. However if you place Christianity and Judaism, there is no such a gap. Race, color and geography has helped such other races to get together and form such a coalition that is not helping whatsoever any Islam propaganda to grow. As a result, Islam has become a religion to be vanished. Or, allow a coexistence in a peaceful respectful way between all human beings. If Muslims or Islam is not willing to change their views to not killing others for any religious reason, they should be hold responsible by the UN or the world governments to a trail to change the main basic fundamental of their beliefs. Modifying their main laws should be a start, for example changing what the Koran says about Jihad should be the first thing to do. Jihad should be banned in Koran.

March 30, 2002, India- two suicide bombers attacked a temple, Raghunath, in Jammu in India. 11 people dead and 20 injured. March 31- 2002, Israel- 16 Israeli civilian were killed (plus the Palestinian bomber) and more than 40 injured in an attack held by Hamas militants. Haifa, the Israeli city was the theatre, again, of mass murder, when a Palestinian Hamas suicide bomber detonated his bomb, during the Passover vacation in Israel, inside the Matza restaurant, killing innocent people, including two families who were completely wiped out. April 10- 2002, Israel- 8 dead and 19 injured, plus the bomber, were all fatalities for the Yagur Junction. Responsibility taken by Hamas. The bomber, a Palestinian militant. April 11- 2002, Tunisia- Djerba was the theatre of a suicide bombing, claimed by Al-Qaeda, killing 19 and injuring more than 30 people from different nationalities, 14 Germans, 3 Tunisians, and 2 French. After the incident, which initially was seen as an accident, it became clear that it was the work of a terrorist Islamic organization. In March 2003, five people were arrested in Spain charged on financing the operation, and the following month, a German man named Christian Ganczarski was arrested in Paris and sentenced to 18 years in prison for his connection to the bombing. April 12- 2002, Israel- Jerusalem, another suicide bombing by a Palestenian bomber, killing himself and other 6 and wounding around 104 people. Responsibility been claimed by Al-Aqsa Martyrs' Brigades.

The bomber was, again, female, 17 years old, at Mahane Yehuda Market, Jerusalem.

Two conclusions to pinpoint to. Anybody, regardless of their nationalities, or gender could became terrorist. Examples are being proved throughout the German terrorist who was part of the Ghriba synagogue Tunisian bombing attack, and the female who blew herself at Mahane Yehuda Market, Jerusalem.

May 7- 2002, Israel- Rishon LeZion bombing has been claimed by Hamas, terrorist organization, killing 16, including the attacker, a Palestinian suicide bomber, and wounding 57 people. The bomber was a Palestinian-Arab Ibrahim Sarahne, married to a Ukrainian prostitute, the wife was caught and convicted for participating in the attack by taking and delivering the bomber to the site of the attack. She was sentenced to 20 years, then released at the end of 2011, as part of a prisoner exchange between Israel and Hamas.

In the other side of the world, the following day, May 8- 2002, Pakistan- Karachi bus bombing claimed the lives of 13, and 40 injured. It was part of many attacks to Westerners in Pakistan during the year 2002. The attack, according to Pakistani and French governments at the time was the work of Al-Qaeda in Pakistan to intimidate any actions taken by western countries in such country. Pakistan was, and still, a big and important state supporting groups of terrorism. Supports are of all levels, mostly training fields for such radicalism to grow and extend all over the world. The bomb was detonated by a man driving a car and stopping next to a bus outside the Sheraton Hotel, in Karachi. 11 Frenchmen engineers working with Pakistan to design a class submarine for the Pakistani Navy were killed in the blast, and two Pakistanis. However, a new investigation has been taking place in France, called "Karachigate" to actually try to link the attack to the halting of commission payments. Therefore, both governments can be implicated. May 14-

2002, India- Three Pakistanis, attacked a tourist bus, near Kaluchak, Jammu and Kashmir, India, killed 31 and injured 47 people. Lashkar-e-Taiba, a Pakistani terrorist organization, held responsible for such atrocity. Its leader, Hafiz Muhammad Saeed, has been arrested after, by Pakistani authorities. July 16- 2002, Israel- Immanuel, West Bank, bus attack, ambush, mass murder, spree killing, bombing and shooting attack, result in the killing of 9 Israeli civilians and non-fatal injuries of 20 others. The terrorists were all three Palestinians disguised as Israeli soldiers, carrying with them grenades, bombs. One of the victims was 11 months old, and another premature infant with just 9 hours, also died. July 17- 2002, Israel- another suicide bombing in the neighborhood in Tel Aviv. The Islamic Jihad of Palestine claimed responsibility for the killing of 5 people, injuring about others 40 innocent people, plus the two suicide bombers.

Three Israelis, one Romanian and one Chinese were the ones victims in the blast carried out by the two Palestinian suicide bombers, who in fact added large amount of shrapnel and nails to maximize the amount of injuries. Such hatred for a false cause. A cause emancipated and justified by Islam. A religion full of hatred to other religions. And, if the Palestinians are fighting for their land, it's understandable in the limit of fighting soldiers not civilians. Civilians haven't done anything wrong. They are just people that live and work to pay their bills. Every terrorist attack that has been explained in this book, actually was killing either civilians or simple security guards or employees in places that happen to be of a Westerners interest. So far, none of the terrorist attacks that have been mentioned here had targeted a military compound or a war zone. The only appellation that could be given to such attacks is, an act of cowards.

July 31- 2002, Israel- A university this time, has been the target of Islam terrorists, precisely the university cafeteria, Mount Scopus campus at Jerusalem. Hamas claimed responsibility, with the killing of 9 civilians, including 5 American students and more less 100 injuries. All civilians. The attackers have been arrested, and serving life sentences in Israeli prisons. August 4- 2002, Israel- another bus attack resulting in the killing of 6 Israeli civilians and 3 soldiers, plus 1 bomber, and the fatality of 38 people, which most were soldiers. Hamas claimed responsibility for the Meron Junction Bus-361 attack, in which the suicide bomber was at the back of the bus, before he detonated the explosive device hidden underneath his clothes. September 19- 2002, Israel, another suicide bombing at Tel Aviv, killed 6 civilians and injured approximately 70. Hamas claimed responsibility for the attack, in which the Palestinian bomber blew himself at the front part of a crowded bus in the middle of Tel Aviv's business district, killing himself too of course.

September 24- 2002, India- an attack at the Akshardham Temple, in Gandhinagar, Gujarat, India. Shootings and bombings using hand grenades and automatic weapons such AK-47 resulted in the death of 33 people, including the two perpetrators, and injuring at least 80 people. Behind the attacks were two Islamic groups, Lashkar-e-Taiba and Jaish-e-Mohammed. The same night of the attacks both attackers have been shot dead. Later on, six people have been arrested, then acquitted of all charges by the Supreme Court, due to lack of evidence and pulled up the Gujarat Police for shoddy investigation in the case. September 29- 2002, Saudi Arabia- another terrorism act attributed to Islamic extremists had resulted in the killing of a German national by a car bomb in central Riyadh. October 2, 17 and 21- 2002, Philippines- Zamboanga city, Philippines, has been the scenario of a series of attacks, by suspected MILF (Moro Islamic Liberation Front), Abu Sayyaf and Jemaah Islamiyah, killing at least 11 and wounding around 180 people. October 6- 2002, France, Yemen- in the Gulf of Aden off of Yemen, an explosive-laden dinghy rammed the French-flagged tanker Limburg, killing one 1 crewman and seriously damaging the ship. October 8- 2002, Kuwait- two Kuwaiti citizens with jihadist ties in Afghanistan launched an attack against United States Marines, stationed in the Faylaka Island, Kuwait. The two attackers have been killed after the assault that took the life of one Marine and injuring another. October 12- 2002, Indonesia- two nightclubs with Western clientele and a US consular office have been attacked by members of Jemaah Islamiyah and al-Qaeda, killing 202 and injuring 240 people. It took place in Bali, Indonesia, with the use of three bombs: a suicide backpack mounted device carried by a suicide bomber, a large car bomb and bomb vest in both the tourist district of Kuta, and outside the U.S. consulate in Denpasar. The attack that killed 202 people include 88 Australians, 38 Indonesians, 27 British, 7 Americans, 6 Swedish, 6 Germans, and people from more than 15 other nationalities. October 21- 2002, Israel- a suicide bomber killed 7 soldiers and 7 civilians and 2 suicide bombers, injuring more than 50 people. Islamic Jihad claimed responsibility of the horrific act. The Karkur junction bus bombing was a suicide attack by the military wing of Palestine Islamic Jihad, the Al-Quds Brigades, and executed by two Palestinians from the West Bank city of Jenin. October 23- 2002, Russia- A hostage situation in Moscow's theatre House of Culture of State Ball-Bearing Plant Number 1 in the Dubrovka area of Moscow about four kilometers south-east of the Moscow Kremlin. A sold-out performance of Nord-Ost, later the crisis took its name from the act, 2002 Nord-Ost siege, was the scene of a heavy attack by 40-50 armed masked men and women drove in a bus to the theater and entered the main hall firing assault rifles in the air, taking between 850 and 900 people hostages. Their demands was the withdrawal of Russian forces from Chechnya and an end to the Second Chechen War, and claimed allegiance to the Islamist militant separatist movement in Chechnya. After a two-and-a-half day siege and the execution of two female hostages, the Russians pumped an undisclosed chemical substance into the building's ventilation system and raided it; killing all 40 attackers, presumably while unconscious; about 130 hostages died, including nine foreigners, due to adverse reactions to the gas.

All but the two females hostages who died by the attackers, were killed by the toxic substance pumped during the siege. A statement was released by the gunmen in which they declared they willingness to die for their cause in the name of "their god" Allah. It says: "... Allah has given us the right of freedom and the right to choose our destiny. And the Russian occupiers have flooded our land with our children's blood. ... And therefore we have decided to die here, in Moscow. And we will take with us the lives of hundreds of sinners". End of quote. More than 170 dead and more than 700 injured by those Islamists. October 27- 2002, Israel- Sonol gas station bombing in which Hamas has claimed responsibility took the lives of 3 soldiers and about 18 injured, mostly soldiers. The attacker was a young Palestinian wearing an explosive belt that detonated after he was being shot, killing three Israeli soldiers. November 21- 2002, Israel- Kiryat Menachem bus bombing; killing 11 and wounding 50 in which Hamas claimed responsibility. The attacker was a Palestinian suicide bomber, wearing a belt packed with explosives and shrapnel. November 24- 2002, India- the second attack on the Raghunath Temple in Jammu in India in the same year, when two suicide Islamic bombers stormed the temple and killed 14 devotees and injured 45. India blamed a Pakistan-based militant group for the attacks, Lashkar-e-Taiba. November 28- 2002, Kenya, Israel- the target of the Mombasa attacks was to kill Israelis at an Israeli-owned hotel and a plane. The attacks were simultaneously carried out by a car bomb at the hotel site and surface-to-air missile fired at a chartered Boeing 757 airliner owned by Israel-based Arkia Airlines as it took off from Moi International airport, but missed to hit the plane. An all-terrain vehicle crashed through a barrier outside the Paradise Hotel and blew up, killing 13 (3 Israelis, 10 Kenyans) and injuring 80 people.

During the year 2002, the world had witnessed the total of 45 Islamic terrorist attacks, with more than 795 deaths and more than 2847 injured victims.

January 5- 2003, Israel- another attack in Tel Aviv resulting in 23 civilians dead and more than 100 wounded. A bus station suicide bombing, in which responsibility has been claimed by Al-Aqsa Martyrs Brigades, a Palestinian militant group. Two Palestinians suicide bombers blew themselves in a crowded area in Tel Aviv outside the Tel Aviv Central Bus Station. February 20- 2003, Saudi Arabia- 1 dead; an American employee of a British multinational defense company, security and aerospace company headquartered in London in the United Kingdom and with operations worldwide, was shot to death in his car in Riyadh. February 28- 2003, Pakistan- an attack on U.S. consulate in Karachi. Gunmen killed two officers and wounded five other officers and civilian in front of the consulate. 2 dead and 5 wounded. March 5- 2003, Israel- Haifa bus 37 suicide bombing. 17 dead and 53 wounded were among the causalities caused by Hamas attack. April 30- 2003, Israel- another suicide claimed by Hamas and Al Aqsa Martyrs took the lives of 3 Israeli civilians and injured more than 50 civilians. May 1- 2003, Saudi Arabia- a man dressed in a Royal Saudi Navy uniform penetrated an American base and shot to death an American. May 12- 2003, Saudi Arabia- 19 men believed to be members of Al-Qaeda planned attacks on Riyadh. Two suicide attacks were carried out, killing 39 people and wounding over 160 when bombs went off at three compounds in Riyadh- Dorrat Al Jadawel, Al Hamra Oasis Village, and the Vinnell Corporation Compound. May 12- 2003, Chechnya- the Znamenskoye Grozny suicide bombing perpetuated by Caucasus Emirate Islamic Group, responsible for the deaths of 59 people and injuring about 200. Three rebel suicide bombers, including two women, drove a truck bomb into a local government administration and the Federal Security Service of the Russian Federation directorate complex, killing and injuring innocent civilians. May 16- 2003, Morocco- Casablanca, the economic capital of Morocco was the scene of several attacks by an Islamic Jihadist group called Salafia Jihadia, killing 45 people including the 12 terrorists and injuring more than 100 people. They were the deadliest terrorist attacks in the country's history. 4 bombs took place in different areas by 14 bombers wearing explosives attacked the guard at "Casa de Espana" restaurant, a Spanish-owned location in the city. They blew themselves up inside the building, killing 20 people, many of them Muslims dining and playing bingo. Then, a hotel has been attacked and bombed, killing the guard and a porter. Another bomber exploded his bomb by Jewish cemetery killing three passerby. In all, 33 civilians died and more than 100 people were injured. After the attacks, a large demonstration was organized by citizens all over the country, refuting the events, carrying banners such as "Say No to Terrorism". They shouted "Down with hate" and "United against Terrorism". May 18, 19 and June 11- 2003, Israel- all bombings in the state of Israel killing a total of 27 and injuring more than 210. French Hill suicide bombing, Afula mall bombing and Davidka Square bus bombing were all carried out and claimed by Islamic Terrorists groups, such as Hamas, Islamic Jihad and Al Aqsa Martyrs Brigades, all Palestinian groups. August 5- 2003, Indonesia- JW Marriot in Jakarta was attacked by a suicide bomber, in which a car bomb was detonated outside the lobby, killing 12 and injuring more than 150. Responsibility for the attack was directed toward two Islamic groups, Jemaah Islamiyah and Al-Qaeda. August 19- 2003, Israel- Hamas organized another suicide bombing, killing 24 civilians; 23 civilians and 1 unborn child, and injuring more than 130 civilians. The Shmuel HaNavi bus bombing was a suicide bombing of a crowded public bus in the Shmuel HaNavi quarter in Jerusalem. August 25- 2003, India- Mumbai was the scene of two car bombings. Both the bombs were planted in parked taxis and exploded during the lunch hour, killing 52 and injuring around 300. Lashkar-e-Toiba, a Kashmir rebel Islamic terrorist Jihadist group; that is still operating from 1986 till present, was blamed for it. September 9- 2003, Israel- two attacks occurred in the same in two different places. Tzrifin bus stop attack was an attack claimed by Hamas, the Palestinian terrorist group, killing 9 soldiers and wounding more than 15 other Israeli soldiers.

It was executed in a bus stop in central Israel next to the military base Tzrifin. Same day another attack was taking place in Jerusalem, by a Palestinian suicide bombing in a coffee shop in the German Colony neighborhood. Seven (7) people were killed in the attack and over 50 were injured. Both attacks were perpetrated by the Hamas terrorist group. October 4, 2003, Israel- the Maxim restaurant suicide bombing was a suicide bombing in the beachfront "Maxim" restaurant in Haifa, Israel. The Palestinian Islamic Jihad claimed responsibility for the attack, executed by a Palestinian suicide bomber, Hanadi Jaradat. The restaurant, which is located at the seafront near the southern boundary of the city of Haifa, was frequently attended by both Arab and Jewish local populations, and was widely seen as a symbol peaceful coexistence in Haifa. That day the suicide bomber took the lives of 21 civilians and injured 51 others. November 8- 2003, Saudi Arabia- 17 people died and around 123 wounded in a truck suicide bombing in west Riyadh. Attackers dressed as policemen, and a car belonging to the Saudi special security forces was used to execute the attack. Also, reports had surged claiming police involvements in the attacks, surprisingly warning the residents living around the area –where the attacks happened- for being too westernized and that their lives were under scrutiny. It was a hidden and sometimes and open secret that many of the religious police supported Osama bin Laden.

Either by helping actively or passively in a terrorist involvement, another government and official entities being involved directly or indirectly in such terrorist attacks.

November 15-20, 2003, Turkey- Istanbul terrorist attacks occurred in a series of two days of events bombings, including the bombings of two synagogues, HSBC Bank and British Consulate. Causalities were 57 civilians dead and over 700 wounded in several operations carried out by the terrorist group Al-Qaeda. Several Britons were killed in the two attacks, while mostly were Turkish citizens. The attacks have been timed to coincide with Bush's visit to the UK. First bombing occurred on November 15, 2003, two trucks carrying bombs slammed into the Bet Israel and Neve Shalom synagogues in Istanbul, Turkey and exploded. The second attack, five days later, on November 20, as US president George W. Bush was in the United Kingdom meeting with UK Prime Minister Tony Blair, two more truck bombs exploded. The bombs were detonated and exploded inside vehicles at the headquarters of HSBC Bank AS (first British bank in Turkey to be established) and the British Consulate.

By such attacks, Al-Qaeda was trying to show the world that any alliance with US is an alliance against Al-Qaeda. Therefore, that explain the attacks on the British entities in Turkey while the President of the United States was visiting to United Kingdom.

The year 2003 had seen 20 terrorist Islamic attacks, with the result of 406 deaths and more than 2,321 injured.

January 10- 2004, Indonesia- Palopo, a bombing at a café place killed 4 people, plus 3 non-fatal injuries, perpetuated by local Islamic militants. The suspects bombers entered the café shop, sat at a table, ordered drinks, then left. After moments, a device exploded at 10:30 p.m. local time, from underneath that same table. Later, after their arrest, one of the responsible for the bombing, confessed calling the attack "part of a jihad against vice in nightclubs and bars". January 14 and 29- 2004, Israel- two other bombings in Israel, first Erez Crossing, Southern District, killing 4 soldiers and security personnel, injuring 10 more, second in Jerusalem, Gaza street bus bombing, killing 11 civilians and wounding more than 50. Both attacks were the work of Hamas and Al-Aqsa Martyrs' Brigades, and executed by two Palestinian suicide jihadist terrorists fanatics. One of the two terrorists was female. She was faking a limp and told security guards at the site, before exploding herself up, that she had a metal plate in her leg which would most likely trigger the alarm. A female soldier was sent to check her, but as the suicide bomber was waiting for the arrival of the female soldier, she managed to infiltrate into the inspection hall, and detonated the hidden explosive, killing herself and another 4 Israeli soldiers. February 6- 2004, Russia- another suicide bombing in Russia, occurred this time at the Moscow Metro train. A suicide bombing responsible for the death of 41 people and injuring between 102 and 120 people. It was executed by a Muslim male suicide bomber, Nikolai Kipkeyev, under a radical group calling itself Muslim Society No 3. Russia blamed Chechen separatists for the Moscow metro attacks. A former Chechen militant Islamist and a leader of the Chechen movement, Shamil Salmanovich Basayev claimed that his organization was responsible for the bombing, also said the cost for the operation was $7,000 U.S. dollars. February 22- 2004, Israel- 8 Israeli civilians were killed in a Jerusalem bus suicide bombing, and another 60 more civilians were injured in another attack by Al-Aqsa Martyrs' Brigades terrorist group. The attack was executed by a Palestinian suicide bomber, during rush hour, when the terrorist got to the bus. He had an explosive device hidden in a backpack which was stuffed with metal scraps to maximize casualties. He waited for the bus to fill up with passengers before he detonated the device, killing innocent people. February 27- 2004, Philippines- Manila Bay was the scene of a horrific terrorist attack, resulting in the deaths of 116 people. The attacks were the work of Abu Sayyaf organization. The bombings occurred at a ferry (SuperFerry 14) sailing out of Manila for Cagayan de Oro City via Bacolod City with 899 recorded passengers and crew aboard. A television set containing an 8 pound TNT bomb had been placed on board in the lower level, more crowded decks.

Abu Sayyaf is Islamic militant group based in and around Philippines, where for more than four decades, from 1991 till present, have been engaged in an insurgency for an independent province in the country. It's a very violent group that allies with Al-Qaeda, and form part of the Islamic State of Iraq and the Levant.

March 9- 2004, Turkey- Two Islamic militants open fire and detonate pipe bombs, killing 1 and injuring 5 others. The attack occurred 911 days after 9/11, killing a waiter at the restaurant where the incident happened. Al-Qaeda organization was behind such atrocity. March 11- 2004, Spain- a local cell of Al-Qaeda in Spain was responsible for the death of 191 people and non-fatal injuries of more than 2,050. Atocha train station was the theatre of mass murder, terrorism and bombing, in Madrid, Spain. Three days before Spain's general election, at a Madrid commuter rail network, the bombings constituted the deadliest terrorist attack in Spanish history and among the worst in the history of Europe. It was the worst attack to occur in Spain, far surpassing the 21 killed and 40 wounded from a 1987 bombing at a supermarket in Barcelona, claimed by ETA, and the worst in Europe since 1988 Lockerbie bombing. During the peak of Madrid rush hour on that day, 11 March 2004, ten explosions occurred aboard four commuter trains (cercanias). At the train Station Atocha, three bombs were exploded between 7:37 and 7:38am. At El Pozo del Tio Raimundo Station, at approximately 7:38, two bombs exploded in various carriages, just as the train was starting to leave the station. Same time, at the Santa Eugenia Station another bomb exploded. Approximately 800 meters from the Atocha Station, around 7:39am, four bombs exploded in different carriages of another train.

The elections were held three days after the bombings. The Party governing Spain was the People's Popular Party (PP). According to the government theory, statements issued shortly after the Madrid attacks identified ETA as the prime suspect, but the group, which usually claims responsibility for its actions, denied any wrongdoing. Political analysts believe ETA's guilt would have strengthened the PP's (right wing party called Popular's Party) chances of being re-elected, as this would have been regarded as the death of a terrorist organization reduced to desperate measures by the strong and rigid anti-terrorist policy of the Aznar's governing PP party administration. On the other hand, an Islamist attack would have been perceived as the direct result of Spain's involvement in Iraq, an unpopular war that had not been approved by the Spanish Parliament.

So basically, because of the unpopularity within the Spanish population in the involvement of Spain in the Iraq war, the government tried to hide all information that could led to a loss in the elections. The public seemed convinced that the Madrid bombings were a result of the Aznar government's alignment with the U.S. and its invasion of Iraq.

According to the European Strategic Intelligence and Security Center, this is the only Islamist terrorist act in the history of Europe where international Islamists collaborated with non-Muslims. The Spanish judiciary stated that a group of Moroccan, Syrian, and Algerian Muslims and two Guardia Civil and Spanish police informants were suspected of having carried out the 11 March attacks.

Although they had no role in the planning or implementation, some Spanish miners who sold the explosives to the terrorists were also arrested.

Another manipulation of the truth proving a government willingness to do whatever it takes to hide the truth from people. A weakness that terrorists can use for their own benefits. This kind of manipulation has to stop whatever the consequences are. The main goal is to stop such attacks, and politics should not be an excuse to any wrongdoing. Before the attacks the PP were up by 5 percent in the polls. Afterwards, the Socialist Party, let by Jose Luis Rodriguez Zapatero, ended up winning the election by 5%. He claimed that the PP government erased all of the computer files related to the Madrid bombings, leaving only the documents on paper.

Former Spanish Prime Minster Jose M. Aznar claimed in 2011 that the current head of Tripoli Military Council was suspected of complicity in the 2004 Madrid bombings. So, how can a suspected Terrorist still be in power? Very strange. This can't be tolerated, and any person suspected of terrorism should be held responsible to answer all their actions. And more importantly, not to be able to hold any important and key position in any government.

March 14- 2004, Israel- Hamas and Fatah claimed responsibility for the attack that killed 10 people and wounded 16, in a suicide bombing at Port of Ashdod in Ashdod, Israel. Both Palestinian terrorist groups used two 18-years-olds Palestinian suicide bombers, who were wearing explosive belts hidden underneath their clothes to explode inside the port compound. April 21, May 1, May 29-30, June 6, June 8, June 13- 2004, Saudi Arabia- 6 simultaneous attacks; car bomb explodes outside a Saudi Police building, killing 5 and injuring 148 people; four militants entered the offices of Texas-based ABB petrochemical plant, and started shooting, killing 7; four Al-Qaeda linked militants attacked two oil industry installations and a residential compound in Al-Khobar, killing 22 and injuring 25; June 6: two BBC journalist were attacked by Al Qaeda followers while filming al Qaeda safe house in Al-Suwaidi, Riyadh; on June 8, an American employee of an international private military company based in the United States specializing in military training, logistics and support in the form of weapon system, Vinnell Corp. was killed in Riyadh by a terrorist act. And on June 13, another American, Paul Marshall Johnson, was kidnapped at a fake police checkpoint. He was kidnapped by Al-Qaeda in the Arabian Peninsula. The group posted a video of a blindfolded Johnson on an Islamist website June 15 and threatened to kill him unless all Al-Qaeda prisoners were released from Saudi jails within 72 hours. After the video release, United States and Saudi Arabia asserted that they would not comply with the kidnappers' demands. On June 18, news and photographs posted on the internet reported that Johnson had been decapitated.

July 28, August 1, 2004, Iraq- in the July attack, a car bomb was placed targeting civilian population. A suicide bombing occurred next to a local market and a police station on July 28, in Baquba, killing 69 and injuring dozens of people. On August, in Baghdad, car bombings of various churches occurred in many places around the city, leaving the death toll of at least 12 and injuring 71 people. August 3- 2004, Saudi Arabia- an Irish national was shot and killed in Riyadh, by a fanatic Islamist terrorist. August 21, 2004, Bangladesh- over 300 people injured and 24 deaths occurred during a grenade attack that took place at an anti-terrorism rally organized by Awami League on Bangadandhu Avenue on 21 August 2004. The attack was carried out after a speech given to a 20,000 people protesting blasts against the party's workers in Sylhet. As Hasina, the sheikh, finished her speech, a total of 13 grenades were thrown into the crown from the rooftops of nearby buildings, killing innocent people and injuring hundreds including Awami League chief Sheikh Hasina. Harkat-ul-Jihad-al-Islami, an Islamic fundamentalist organization most active in South Asian countries of Pakistan, Bangladesh and India since 1990s, was responsible for the act. August 31- 2004, Russia- another Moscow metro bombing resulted in the death of 10 and wounding 50 people when a female suicide bomber blew herself up outside Rizhskaya metro station. The deaths included the bomber and her accomplice, Nikolay Kipkeev, the head of an Islamic militant group Karachay Jamaat from the republic of Karachay-Cherkessia, as the bomb apparently exploded prematurely while the two were standing in the entrance hall of the metro station. August 31- 2004, Israel- a bus bombing killing 16 and injuring more than a 100 people took place Beersheda, Israel. Two Palestinian assailants were responsible for two suicide bombings, both claimed by Hamas, carried out nearly simultaneously aboard commuter buses in the Beersheda location.

September 1-3, 2004, Russia- a hostage situation took place at a school in Beslan, North Ossetia-Alania; Russia. A situation with three days hostage involved the capture of over 1,000 people as hostages (including 777 children), and ended with the death of at least 385 people. The hostage takers were the Riyadus-Salikhin Battalion, a small "martyr" force of Islamic suicide attackers, sent by the Chechen warlord Shamil Basayev, who demanded recognition of the independence of Chechnya in UN and Russian withdrawal from Chechnya. At least 385 hostages were killed, including 186 children, with a non-fatal injuries of approximately 783. To end the standoff, on the third day, Russian security forces stormed the building with the use of tanks, incendiary rockets and other heavy weapons.

The Beslan school hostage crisis was another example of how cruel the Islamic Jihadism can be; killing children to gain political power. It proves that such ideology doesn't respect age, race or gender. Islamic Terrorists could harm and kill anybody even children. It is unhuman, and to live in peace it should be stopped and eradicated from its origin.

September 9, 2004, Indonesia- a suicide bomber exploded a one-ton car bomb, which was packed into a small delivery van, outside the Australian embassy at Kuningan District, South Jakarta killing 9 people including the suicide bomber and wounding over 150. Responsibility for the attack was claimed by Jemaah Islamiyah, an organization that allies itself to Taliban and Al-Qaeda. It is a Southeast Asian militant Islamist terrorist group dedicated to the establishment of Daulah Islamiyah (regional Islamic caliphate) in Southeast Asia. An organization which has also claimed responsibility for multiple attacks including the 2002 Bali bombing. After the bombing the group posted a statement saying: "We decided to settle accounts with Australia, one of the worst enemies of God and Islam … and Mujahedeen brother succeeded in carrying out a martyr operation with a car bomb against the Australian embassy… it is the first of series of attacks. … We advise Australians in Indonesia to leave the country or else we will transform it into a cemetery for them. Our Jihad (holy war) will continue until the liberation of the land of Muslims". Hatred, hatred and hatred toward people, and this is totally unacceptable for a religion to be advertising. Statements like that does nothing positive but create conflicts and divide races and worlds apart. September 15- 2004, Saudi Arabia- a British national working for the Marconi Company was shot to death in his car in Riyadh. October 7- 2004, Egypt- targeting foreigners in a touristic area of Sinai Peninsula have killed 34 and wounded 171 people. Three bombs occurred on the night of 7 October, against the Hilton Taba and campsites used by Israelis in Ras al-Shitan. November 2- 2004, the murder of Theo van Gogh by Amsterdam-born jihadist Mohammed Bouyeri was another example of how wrong Islam is regarding the concept of Jihad. There is no explanation or excuse allowed to kill anybody because of their race or religion. It was a cowardly act. November 13- 2004, Indonesia- the bombing occurred at Poso, Central Sulawesi, Indonesia. It was a terrorist act that targeted a bus travelling to the majority Christian village of Silancak. The bomb, an improvised device, exploded while the minibus was stopped at a market in Poso. 6 deaths and 3 injured were the causalities of local Islamist militants. December 6- 2004, Saudi Arabia- five militants attacked the American consulate in Jeddah, killing 9 and wounding about 10, perpetrated by suspected local Islamic militants.

2004 had 28 attacks, at least 958 deaths and more than 3888 injured.

January 13- 2005, Israel- Karni border crossing attack; 6 Israeli civilians plus 3 attackers died and 5 Israelis injured in an attack perpetuated by Hamas, the Al Aqsa Martyrs Brigades and the Popular Resistance Committees. It was a suicide bombing at the pedestrian/cargo terminal Karni Crossing located on the Israeli Gaza Strip barrier. February 14- 2005, Lebanon- the assassination of Rafic

Hariri, the former Prime Minister of Lebanon, was killed along with 21 others when 1,000 kilograms of TNT exploded near his motorcade, close to the St. George Hotel in Beirut. TNT is considered to be the standard measure of strength of bombs and other explosives. In chemistry, TNT is used to generate charge transfer salts. TNT, or more specifically 2,4,6-Trinitrotoluene, is a chemical compound with the formula $C6H2(NO2)3CH3$. This yellow-colored solid is sometimes used as a reagent in chemical synthesis, but it is best known as a useful explosive material with convenient handling properties. It is mostly used by terrorists to explode themselves in suicide bombings. Hariri was opposed to the presence and plan of extension to the term of Lebanese President Emile Lahoud. Syria had extensive military and intelligence influence in Lebanon at the time of Hariri's murder, but Damascus claimed repeatedly it had no knowledge of the bombing. In August 2004, Syrian President Bashar al-Assad threatened Hariri, saying "Lahoud represents me … if you and Chirac want me out of Lebanon, I will destroy Lebanon." Chirac, former French President was a close personal friend of Hariri. The later was known for his opposition to the support that Damascus and specially President Assad had for Lebanon president Lahoud. A United Nations report sponsored by the US and UK found converging evidence of Syrian and Lebanese involvement in the attack against Hariri. On December 2005, former Syrian vice-president Abdul Halim Khaddam in a televised interview implicated President Assad in the assassination and said that Assad personally threatened Hariri in the months before his death. Following Hariri's death, there were several other bombings and assassinations against anti-Syrian figures. February, 25- 2005, Israel- a nightclub called Stage was the scene pf a suicide bombing that resulted in the death of 5 Israelis and wounding more than 50 Israelis. The Islamic Jihad claimed its responsibility for the attack, that been prepared by a Palestinian suicide bomber who blew himself up outside the "Stage" beachfront nightclub in Tel Aviv, Israel. May 28- 2005, Indonesia-the Tentena market bombings occurred in Tentena, Central Sulawesi, Indonesia. Two improvised devices, set to explode 15 minutes apart, detonated during the morning at a market in the center of Tertena, killing 22 and injuring around 90 more people. Among the fatalities a 3-year-old-boy. Perpetrators were local Islamic militants with purported links to the group Jemaah Islamiyah. July 5- 2005, India- five terrorists attacked the makeshift Ram temple at the site of destroyed Badri Mosque in Ayodha, India. Following the demolition of the Badr Masjid in 1992, a makeshift temple had been constructed at the Ram Janmabhoomi site. According to Hindu mythology, the site was the birthplace of the God-king Rama. On that July, the heavily guarded Ram was attacked by heavily armed terrorists. The terrorists were from the terrorist organization Lashkar-e-Toiba, and believed to have entered India through Nepal. All five were shot dead in the ensuing gunfight with the Central reserve Police Force, while one civilian died in the grenade attack the terrorists launched in order to breach the cordoned wall. Such attack was an example of the clash of religions, over worthless religious values. Total 6 dead. July 7- 2005, England- the country witnessed one of the most devastating attacks in their soil, since the 1988 Lockerbie bombing. Four Islamist extremists, Hasib Hussain, Mohammad Sidique Khan, Germaine Lindsay (Jamaican converted to Islam, one of the rare and few Terrorists with no Muslim relatives background) and Shehzad Tanweer, were responsible for the death of 56 people including themselves and more than 700 injured in a series of coordinated suicide bomb attacks in central London Underground trains and bus, where they targeted civilians using the public transport system during the morning rush hour. The explosions were caused by homemade organic peroxide-based devices packed into backpacks. They occurred just one day after London had won its bid to host the 2012 Olympic Games. Two of the bombers made videotapes describing their reasons for becoming what they called "soldiers" and martyrs for God: "Our religion is Islam, obedience to the one true Gid and following the footsteps of the final prophet messenger... I myself make dua (pray) to Allah... to raise me amongst whom I love like the prophets, the messengers, the martyrs and todays heroes like our beloved Sheikh Osama Bin Laden,... and all other brothers and sisters that are fighting in the ... of this cause. ... What have you witnessed now is only the beginning of a string of attacks that will continue and become stronger until you pull your forces out of Afghanistan and Iraq. And until you stop your financial and military support to America and Israel". After reading such message, it seems clear that those terrorists have been going through some kind of brainwash to let them decide the faith and killing of other people for no logical reason. It's all a lie elaborated and executed by ignorant people calling themselves martyrs and killing innocent people. The only thing they have done correctly is leaving this planet without them on it.

By suiciding and killing other people, those terrorists don't help in any way that the war in Iraq will stop. The US troop withdraw from those lands, but the terrorists still go with their plans of killing innocent people. Afghanistan, Iraq or Palestine are only excuses for those people to create chaos and kill innocent people. They are bad by nature, and nothing will change their mind, even with the Israeli withdrawal from Palestine. It won't change their concept toward westerners. Those four terrorists' demands were with no value and just a false excuse to get support from their followers. It's a total ignorance and with no concrete results, except making it worse for other believers of the same religion "Muslims". And it's becoming a necessity for people who claim to believe in Islam to change their beliefs and let that religion Islam sink to its end. The only way to save such religion is to modify its contents, and give the same rights to anybody with other beliefs to cohabitate in a peaceful manner. Changes should be oriented first to the idea regarding martyrs concept, it should be erased from such religion. There should be no justification or explanation to kill somebody because of their beliefs, westerner or easterner. The Koran should be either modified or getting rid of. Actually, such book wasn't the creation of God, and such Prophet Mahomet was not honest with his words and the book itself. It was the creation of a person for his own benefits.

July 12- 2005, Israel- a mall suicide bombing that killed 5 and injured more than 90 people was claimed by Palestinian Islamist militant organization Islamic Jihad. A bombing that occurred for the second time in the same mall, HaSharon mall, located in the city of Netanya, Israel. During the evening of July 12, 2005, a Palestinian suicide bomber, who was wearing hidden explosives underneath his clothes, detonated himself on a pedestrian crossing, after approaching a group of four young women, who were crossing the road. Three women were killed in the attack. The explosion occurred in a busy intersection outside the mall during the evening rush hour, resulting in lot of casualties and damages to other cars and buildings close by. After the attack the local police stated the suicide bomber carried around 10 kg of explosives, as well as nails and metal pellets, on an explosive belt strapped to his body.

July 23- 2005, Egypt- Sharm el-Sheikh was the place of a series of terrorist attacks perpetuated by an Islamist organization, Abdullah Azzam Brigades and Bedouin militants, killing 88 people and wounding around 150 people, the majority of them Egyptians, making the attack the deadliest terrorist action in Egypt's history. Arrested suspects claimed to have been motivated by the War in Iraq, and claimed to have ties to Al-Qaeda. The suicide bombings occurred at a market in downtown Sharm el-Sheikh and the Ghazala Gardens hotel, trying to damage the country's economy by disrupting tourism, a major industry. The attacks took place in the early morning, at a time when many tourists and locals were still out at restaurants, cafes and bars. There were three bombs, very powerful, shaking windows miles away, and fire could be seen rising from the explosion sites. Among the casualties, which mostly were

Egyptians, there were 11 Britons, 6 Italians, 4 Turks, 2 Germans, one Czech, one Israeli, and one American. Other casualties, dead and injured, included foreign visitors from France, Kuwait, the Netherlands, Qatar, Russia, and Spain.

August 17- 2005, Bangladesh- at least 115 people were injured and 2 killed in a series of 500 small-bombs that exploded in 62 out of 63 districts of Bangladesh. A terrorist organization, Jama'atul Mujahideen Bangladesh claimed responsibility for the bombings. The group, led by Shaykh Abdur Rahman and Siddiqur Rahman (known as Bangla Bhai), is alleged to be affiliated with Al Qaeda. Another terrorsit group, Harkat-ul-Jihad al-Islami, was associated with the first group in executing the coordinated attack. The main perpetrators of the bombings, two terrorists, Bangla Bhai and Shaykh Abdur Rahman, were captured, convicted and were executed by hanging on March 30 2007. 5 other suspects were sentenced to death and one to 20 years in prison for their part in the bomb attacks in Bogra. By 2013, in connection to the bombings, different courts have sentenced 58 people to death and 150 were sentenced to life prison and 300 others were sentenced to various terms in prisons. Following the bombings, both groups were banned by the Government of Bangladesh.

October 1- 2005, Indonesia- Main square in central Kuta, warungs along the Jimbaran beach were attacked by suicide and car bombings, resulting in the killing of 20 people and injuring more than 100 others. The 2005 Bali bombings were a series of terrorist bombings perpetuated by Jemaah Islamiyah, a Southeast Asian militant Islamist terrorist group, with a strength of 5,000 terrorist militants, dedicated to create a regional Islamic caliphate. Following this attack, the named group was added to the UN Security Council Resolution 1267 as a terrorist group linked to al-Qaeda or the Taliban. The three bombers also died in the attack, adding more casualties.

October 26- 2005, Israel- Islamic Jihad movement, operating from 1987 till present, is a Palestinian Islamist terror group formed in 1981 whose objective is the destruction of Israel and the establishment of a sovereign, Islamic Palestinian state. On that day, October 26, 2005, the organization was the responsible of the Hadera Market suicide bombing. 7 Israeli civilians dead and 55 other Israeli civilians injured were the casualties of such attack, executed by a Palestinian suicide bomber, who wore an explosive belt hidden underneath his clothes. He approached the open market in the small Israeli coastal town of Hadera, and detonated the explosive device at the market. The timing was well calculated when the market place was busy with shoppers in advance of a Jewish Holiday, with many stocking up for the weekend.

October 29- 2005, India- 62 people killed and around 210 injured in series of bombing at two markets and a bus, in Delhi, India. Three bombings came only two days before the important festival of Diwali, which is celebrated by Hindus, Sikhs, and Jains.

Several of the terrorist attacks occurred during significant holidays, before, during or after. It doesn't mean that future attacks will be planned around those days. Terrorists are working in a random turf, and they have all the time to decide when and where they can execute their barbaric acts. The 2005 Delhi bombings were perpetuated by the Kashmir separatist Islamic terrorist group Lashkar-e-Taiba. The first blast took place in the main bazaar of Paharganj near the New Delhi Railway Station. The second blast took place near a bus in Govindpuri area in the southern part of the city. And, the third blast, which was within seconds of the second explosion, took place in South Delhi's busy Sarojni Nagar market.

October 30- 2005, Indonesia- three underage girls, one 15 and two 17 young girls were beheaded by Muslim militants in the Poso region on the Indonesian island of Sulawesi for being Christians. Central Sulawesi has experienced Muslim-Christian violence in recent years. The most serious violence occurred between 1998 and into 2000. Over 1000 people were killed in violence, riots, and tens of thousands were expelled from their homes. After a period of relative calm, hostilities were reignited by rumors that a Muslim girl had been raped by Christian. Thousands of Muslims and Christians died in the following year, and more than 60,000 families are reported to have fled their homes. After the October attacks, Later on, three men were arrested convicted of the crime, one being sentenced to 20 and two others to 14 years.

November 9- 2005, Jordan- Al-Qaeda in Iraq was responsible for Amman's suicide bombings attacks, that killed 60 and injured around 115 people. A series of coordinated bomb attacks on three hotel lobbies in Amman. The Grand Hyatt Hotel, the Radisson SAS Hotel, and the Days Inn were the three hotels where the explosions started around 8:50 pm local time. One of the bombs exploded in a Ballroom, Radisson SAS Philadelphia hotel, where a wedding hosting hundreds of guests was taking place. Police Jordanians confirmed later that the attackers were Iraqi and that there were three suicide bombers. On November 13, king Abdullah of Jordan announced the arrest of a woman believed to be a fourth would-be suicide bomber, whose explosive belt failed to detonate. Al-Qaeda in Iraq immediately claimed the attack on a website, saying they were trying to hit "American and Israeli intelligence and other Western European governments".

December 5- 2005, Israel- the third HaSharon Mall entrance suicide bombing was a suicide bombing carried out by a Palestinian suicide bomber, who approached the entrance to the Mall in the Israeli coastal city of Netanya. He detonated explosives hidden under his clothes when he approached the guards at the entrance for security inspection. Five (5) people were killed in the attack, and more than 40 Israeli civilians injured. After the attack, the Palestinian Islamist militant organization Islamic Jihad said they were responsible for the attack. December 31- 2005, Indonesia- a nail bomb explodes in a butcher's shop frequented by Christians in Palu, killing 8 and injuring 53.

Year 2005 have witnessed 16 claimed Islamic terrorist attacks, 348 dead, and more than 1,541 injured.

March 2- 2006, Pakistan- a suicide car bomb killed 4 people and injure d30 outside the Marriot Hotel in Karachi, which is close to the American consulate. The bomb was reported to be the most powerful attack of its kind in Karachi. It appears that an American diplomat, Foy, was the direct target of the bomber, who detonated his vehicle in the car park behind the consulate as Foy arrived. March 7- 2006, India- the 2006 Varanasi bombings were a series of bombings that occurred across the Hindu holy city of Varanasi in India on Tuesday, 7 March 2006. At least 28 people are reported to have been killed and as many as 101 others were injured. Targets were Sankat Mochan Hanuman temple and Varanasi Cantonment Railway Station. Perpetrators were Lashkar-e Kahar/Qahab, they claimed responsibility for the attacks. May 30, and April 17, 2006, Israel- two bombings, the first occurred at Kedumim, West Bank, killing 4 civilians. Al-Aqsa Martyrs Brigades claimed responsibility for the suicide bombing. The second attack was at a Tel Aviv shawarma restaurant, killed 11 people and injured around 70 people. It was the work of Islamic Jihad Movement, the Palestinian Islamist terror organization formed in 1981. On that day, a Palestinian suicide bomber approached a crowded fast food restaurant near the old Tel Aviv Central Bus Station in the southern part of the Neve Shaanan neighborhood. The suicide bomber blew himself up when the security guard stationed at the entrance to the restaurant asked him to open his bag for inspection. April 24- 2006, Egypt- Jama'at al-tawhid wal-Jihad, an active terrorist group operated between 1999 till 2004, was a militant Jihadist group led by Jordanian national Abu Musab al-Zarqawi, responsible for the three bomb attacks on the Egyptian resort city of Dahab, in the Sinai Peninsula. The resort town is popular with Western tourists and Egyptians alike during the holiday season. The bombings, which happened at Nelson Restaurant, Aladdin Café and Ghazala Market, were targeting touristic resorts and restaurants. It led to the deaths of 23 people and around 80 injured. April 30, and July 11- 2006, India- both attacks totaled the number of 244 dead and over 700 people injured. The first was Doda massacre, where 35 Hindu civilians have been massacred by terrorists in Doda district in Jammu and Kashmir on 30 April 2006. The second attack in the Indian soil was the Mumbai train bombings, where seven bombs blasts over a period of eleven minutes occurred on the Suburban Railway in Mumbai. The bombs were set off in pressure cookers on trains plying the western line of the Suburban Railway network, two hundreds nine people were killed and over seven hundreds injured.

September 15- 2006, Yemen- 5 people died in two attempted bombings of oil facilities in Yemen, four of them were the attackers.

Year 2006 witnessed the attacks of 8 terrorist Islamic attacks. Under such attacks, the casualties had been 319 dead people and 981 injured.

January 29- 2007, Israel- Eilat bakery bombing was the work of Islamic terrorist groups of al-Aqsa Martyrs' Brigades, Islamic Jihad and Islamic Brigade. A Palestinian suicide bomber from the Gaza Strip infiltrated the northern suburbs of Eilat, Israel, and detonated his bomb, killing 3 people; the bakery's co-owners and an employee. April 18- 2007, Turkey- three employees of the Bible publishing house were attacked, tortured and murdered by five Muslim assailants. The incident happened in the Zirve Publishing House, Malatya, Turkey. Two of the victims were Turkish converts from Islam. The third man was a German citizen. May 13- 2007, India- Indian Mujahideen, is the terrorist group that claimed responsibility for the Jaipur bombings, killing 80 people and injuring more than 216 others. It was a series of nine synchronized bomb blasts that took place within a fifteen minutes gap at various locations in Jaipur, the capital city of the Indian state of Rajasthan, and a tourist destination. A tenth bomb was found and detained. Another suspect group was also to blame, Harkat-ul-Jihad-al-Islami, an organization most active in South Asian countries of Pakistan, Bangladesh and India since the early 1990s. June 30- 2007, Scotland- a suicide attack claimed the life of 1 terrorist bomber, trying to defuse what supposed to be a bomb, 5 people injured. It was a terrorist attack with motives related to extremist Islamic beliefs. Bilal Talal Samad Abdullah, a resident of Houston, outside Glasgow, born in England, was one of the two terrorists behind the 2007 London car bombs plot that been neutralized 36 hours before, and this Glasgow International Airport attack, he was a an Iraqi doctor, and is currently serving a life sentence with a minimum of 32 years. July 10- 2007, Philippines- the 2007 Basilan beheading incident was an armed incident in July 2007 between the Moro Islamic Liberation Front (MILF) rebels and the Philippine Army which led to the execution of 14 to 23 members of the Philippines Marines, among them 11 beheaded in the province of Basilan in the southern Philippines, and injuring 9 others. August 14- 2007, Iraq-Yazidi communities bombings occurred when four coordinated suicide bomb attacks detonated in the Yazidi towns of Qahtaniya and Jazeera, near Mosul, Iraq. 796 killed and 1,562 wounded were the casualties of such terror attack, which has been linked to Al-Qaeda in Iraq. Leaflets were distributed, before the attacks, denouncing Yazidis as "anti-Islamic" and warning them that an attack was imminent. For few months leading up the attack, tensions had been building up in the area, particularly between Yazidis and Sunni Muslims. Some Yazidis living in the area received threatening letters calling them "infidels".

2007 has seen one of the fewer Islamic attacks in years, 6 attacks, but the casualties were still high; 896 dead and 1,792 people injured.

February 4- 2008, Israel- Dimona suicide bombing was an attack executed by two Palestinian assailants, in which al-Aqsa Martyrs' Brigades and the Popular Front for the Liberation of Palestine PFLP claimed responsibility. It resulted in the death of 1 Israeli civilian and injured 9 other Israeli civilians. The PFLP is a secular Palestinian Marxist-Leninist and revolutionary socialist organization founded in 1967 by George Habash. It has consistently been the second-largest of the groups forming the Palestine Liberation Organization (PLO), the largest being Fatah (which the founder was Yasser Arafat, and president is Mahmoud Abbas). PFLP is described as a terrorist organization by United States, Canada, and the European Union. Other countries, such as China, Russia or the United Kingdom do not designate PFLP as a terrorist group.

July 26, September 13 and September 27, 2008, India- In July 26, Ahmedabad bombings were a series of twenty one bomb blasts that hit the city of Ahmedabad, India, in an hour and ten minutes time. It resulted in the killing of 56 people and wounding of more than 200 people. Indian Mujahideen and Harkat-ul-Jihad-al-Islami were the suspected for the massacres. Five minutes before the attacks an e-mail sent to several news agencies with the subject line: "Await 5 minutes for the revenge" in the contents of the e-mail it says: "In the name of Allah the Indian Mujahideen strike again! Do whatever you can, within 5 minutes from now, feel the terror of Death". In September 13, Pakistani extremist groups plant bombs at various places including the India gate, Delhi, India. The explosions resulted in a fatality resumed around 30 people dead and 130 injured. On 27 September, another attack occurred leaving 3 people dead and 23 injured in an explosion in Mehrauli's Electronic market called Sarai. September 20- 2008, Pakistan- Islamabad Marriott Hotel bombing was another deadly attack with explosives detonated outside the hotel, killing at least 54 people, and injuring around 266 others. It was a suicide truck bombing, a dumb truck filled with explosives detonated while it had been stopped at the front hotel barrier for a checkup. October 2008 – January 2009, Iraq- multiple attacks on Christians has resulted in the death of more than 40 people in Mosul, by suspected perpetrators al-Qaeda in Iraq. November 26- 2008, India- Muslim extremists killed at least 166 people and wounded more than 600 others in multiple attacks targeting Jewish and touristic places for four days, began 26 November and lasted until 29 November 2008. The motive was Islamic extremism, with psychological indoctrination to Islamist ideas, including imagery of atrocities suffered by Muslims in India, Chechnya, Palestine, and across the globe. Their basic combats were associated with those taken by Lashkar-e-Taiba. Ten members of Lashkar-e-Taiba terrorist organization carried out the 12 coordinated attacks, shooting and bombing lasting four days.

2008 had seen 7 terrorist Islamic attacks, 350 dead and 962 injured.

June 1- 2009, United States of America- al-Qaeda in the Arabian Peninsula recruited an American born terrorist Islamist to carry out a drive-by shooting attack on soldiers in front of a United States military recruiting office in Little Rock, Arkansas. One (1) dead and one (1) non-fatal injury. June, 18- 2009, Somalia- a suicide car bomb had killed 35 people in an attack at the front gate of the Medina Hotel, Beledweyne, Hiiraan, Somalia. The al-Shabaab group claimed responsibility for the attack. It is a terrorist group, operating from 2006 till present, a jihadist terrorist group based in east Africa. In 2012, it pledged allegiance to the militant Islamist organization Al-Qaeda. July 17- 2009, Indonesia- suicide bombers hit the Marriott and minutes later the Ritz-Carlton in Mega Kuningan, South Jakarta, Indonesia. 9 people died and 53 others injured in an attack perpetuated by Jemaah Islamiyah, the Southeast Asian militant Islamist terrorist group. November 5- 2009, United States of America- Fort Hood shooting, at Fort Hood near Killeen, Texas. Nidal Hasan, a U.S. Army major and psychiatrist, fatally shot 13 people and injured more than 30 others, in a shooting that caused more casualties than any other on an American military base. Born in the United States, Hassan is a practicing Muslim who, according to his cousin, Nader Hassan, a lawyer in Virginia, said that Nidal Hassan's opinion turned against the United States after he heard stories from his patients, who had returned from fighting in Afghanistan and Iraq. Because of what Hassan said was discrimination and his deepening anguish about serving in a military that fought against Muslims, he told some of his families that he wanted to leave the military. He had ties with the Yemen-based imam Anwar al-Awlaki, with whom he had been e-mailing for a while. Hassan was found guilty on all 13 counts of premeditated murder and 32 counts of attempted premeditated murder on August 23, 2013, and was sentenced to death on August 28, 2013.

2009 had 4 known Islamic terrorist attacks, 58 deaths, 89 injured.

During the first 10 years of the 21st century, Islamic Terrorism had claimed the lives of more than 7,305 who died victims from tens of terrorist attacks, and more than 21,024 people injured. In the era from the beginning of 2000 till the end of 2009, there were more than 150 Islamic attacks related to jihadism, killing not only Westerners but also other races, citizens from countless countries and religious fanatics. Basically, everybody can be targeted, regardless of their race, gender, religion, origin, color or age, anywhere on earth. Shame on anybody who kills others for whatever reason.

The 2010th

January 7, 2010- Egypt- some few radicalist Muslims carried out a terrorist attack targeting Coptic Christians, in the Egyptian city of Nag Hammadi. It was an attack executed by Muslin gunmen in front of the Nag Hammadi cathedral, as Coptic Christians were leaving the church after celebrating the midnight Christmas mass. The massacre resulted in the murder of 11, and injuries of other 11 people. Seven Copts and one Muslim bystander died during the massacre, and nine other Copts were confirmed to be wounded. The incident was one of the most serious outbreaks of anti-Christian violence in Egypt, and the worst since murder of 21 Coptic in Kosheh in January 2000. Coptic Christians represent 15% to 20% of a population of over 80 million Egyptians. The Coptic community has been targeted by terrorism throughout the past by Islamic extremists, and has faced varying degrees of discriminatory government policies. Since the 1970s, the rise of Islamist movements in Egypt has let to sectarian violence. It had been seen as forms of communal violence between different sects of one particular mode of ideology or religion, in this case between Copts and Muslims within the same nation. Egyptian Police have been accused of delaying their response to reports of fighting and then simply arresting more Christians than Muslims. Disputes over land and inter-faith relationships have sometimes split communities along religious lines. Other forms of anti-Christian discrimination in Egypt include discrimination in hiring in the public sector and staff appointments to public universities, prohibition from studying at Al-Azhar Univesity (Cairo university, founded in 970), and barring from certain jobs such as Arabic language teachers.

This concept; this way of interacting between two different religions or races in Egypt is not unique only to that part of the world. It is a worldwide phenomenon stopping the world from heading to a better socio-human development. It hurts in all kind of ways any cohabitation between races. Therefore, it create a hatred atmosphere between people, and can lead to violence.

February 3, 2010, Pakistan- 8 people were killed and 70 injured in the 2010 Lower Dir suicide bombing, in Khyber Pakhtunkhwa, Pakistan. The casualties included three American soldiers. Tehrik-i-Talibal Pakistan claimed responsibility for the bombing. March 3- 2010, Iraq- Al-Qaeda in Iraq was responsible for a series of three bombings in Baqubah, Iraq, that killed at least 33 people and injured 55 others. It was a series of two car bombs and one suicide bomb at the hospital where some of the wounded were being treated. A fourth bomb was found near the hospital and defused. March 29- 2010, Russia- another Moscow Metro bombings, caused by Islamic Terrorist group Caucasus Emirate, and Al-Qaeda as another suspected perpetrator, were carried out by two women during the rush hour, at two stations of the metro. The bombs killed 40 people and injured over 102 others. The bombings were the latest in a series of attacks in Russia since 1994, many attributed to Chechen militants or to the Caucasus Emirate. May 10- 2010, Iraq- different locations has been the targets of many coordinated bomb detonations, suicide car bombings, targeted killings and shooting in one day throughout Iraq. All attacks executed by the Islamic Terrorist organization Al-Qaeda Iraq, targeting people at cities as Baghdad, Mosul, Basra, Fallujah, Iskandariyah, Al Tarmia, Suwayrah, and Samarra. A total of more than 114 people died and more than 350 injured, the highest death toll for a single day in Iraq in 2010. May 28- 2010, Pakistan- an Islamic Terrorist group, Tehrik-i-Taliban Pakistan, is an organization of various Islamist militant groups based in the northwestern Federally Administrated Tribal Areas along the Afghan border in Pakistan, referred to as the Pakistani Taliban and operating from 2007 till present, was responsible for the deadly attack, that killed 87 people and injured more than 120 people. The attacks occurred in Lahore, Punjab, Pakistan, during Friday prayers, against two mosques of the minority Ahmadiyya Community. With this attack, it has been proven that Islamic Terrorist attacks don't differentiate themselves from attacking even mosques.

July 11- 2010, Uganda- Al-Shabaab, an Islamist militia based in Somalia that has ties to Al-Qaeda, claimed responsibility for the suicide bombing, carried out against crowds watching a screening of the 2010 FIFA World Cup Final match at two locations in Kampala, the capital city of Uganda, on July 11. The attacks left 74 dead victims and 70 injured.

July 15- 2010, Iran- the Zahedan bombings were two suicide bombings, that targeted Shia worshippers in Iran, including member of the Revolutionary guards. Jundallah, Soldiers of God, also known as People's Resistance Movement of Iran, was the responsible for the attacks. It is a terrorist militant organization based in Balochistan, an unstable province in the Islamic Republic of Pakistan, which claim to be fighting for "Equal rights of Sunni Muslims in Iran". Shia is a branch of Islam which holds that the Islamic prophet Muhammad's proper successor as Caliph was his son-in-law and cousin Ali ibn Abi Talib. Shia Islam primarily contrasts with Sunni Islam, the latest followers whose adherents believe that Muhammad's father-in-law Abu Bakr, not Ali ibn Abi Talib, was his proper successor. The July 15, 2010 two suicide bombings resulted in more than 27 deaths and more than 270 people injured. So basically, the whole religion is split because of this non sense that happened more than 15 centuries ago. People still got killed for that division. It explains how this religion is messed up.

A brief explanation of those two fractions of Islam is important to explain. So, the Shia branch of Islam, like said before, holds that the Islamic prophet Muhammad's proper successor as Caliph was his son-in-law and cousin Ali ibn Abi Talib. Not Abu- Bakr his father-in-law. Shia Islam is the second largest branch of Islam, as of 2009, Shia Muslims constituted 10% to 13%, no more than 15%, of the world's Muslim population. Shia Islam is based on the Quran and the message of the Islamic prophet Muhammad attested in hadith recorded by the Shia, and certain books deemed sacred to the Shia. That's why, actually, most Sunni Muslims think that the Shia are very hard headed Muslims and stuck conservatives, because they only interpret —from a limited perception- two sources; the Coran and Hadith, no other interpretations of a foreigner point of view could be given. Shia consider Ali to have been divinely appointed as the successor to Muhammad, and the first Imam. While Sunnis think that the divine intervention was only toward Muhammad, and nobody else. That explain how they (Shia) extend this "Imami" doctrine to Muhammad's family only, the Ahl al-Bayt (the people of the house), and certain individuals among his descendants, known as Imams, who they believe possess special spiritual and political authority over the community. Shia Muslims believe that just as a prophet is appointed by God only, only God has the prerogative to appoint the successor to his prophet. They believe God chose Ali to be Muhammad's successor. Sunni Islam is, in the other side holds that the Islamic prophet Muhammad's first Caliph was his father-in-law Abu Bakr. The latest, actually, was the one elected after Muhammad's death, and Ali was elected fourth, after the death of the third Caliph Othman. As of 2009, Sunni Muslims constituted 87% to 90% of the world's Muslim population. Sunni Islam is the world's largest religious denomination, after Roman Catholicism. Laws for the Sunnis are derived from Quran and binding consensus from six majors hadith collections; they are Sahih Bukhari, Sahih Muslim, Sunan Abu Dawood, Jami al-Tirmidhi, Sunan al-Sughra and Muwatta Malik. They are different but bonded explanations of Islamic laws that govern everyday life issues and any Muslim or human being interaction with each other. They are basically the constitution of the Muslim empire. Laws are generally derived from these basics sources; in addition, Sunni Islam's juristic schools recognize differing methods to derive legal verdicts such as analogical reason, consideration of public welfare and juristic discretion. Sunni is a term derived from Sunnah, meaning "Hadith". The Muslim use of this term refers to the meaning of any saying and living habits of the prophet Muhammad.

The first four caliphs are known among Sunnis as the Rashidun or "Rightly-Guided Ones". Sunni recognition includes the aforementioned Abu Bakr as the first, Umar who established the Islamic calendar as the second, Othman as the third, and Ali as the fourth. The sequence of events of the 20th century has led to resentments in some places as the Levant, Mesopotamia, the Balkans and the Caucasus.

August 17, 25 and October 31, 2010, Iraq- Islamic State of Iraq, a terrorist group, referred as al-Qaeda in Iraq, active from 2006 till 2013, was responsible for the 17 August 2010 Baghdad bombings, where two bombings attacks resulted on the death of more than 69 and 169 injures. On 25 August, a string of attacks in Iraqi cities targeting mostly Iraqi security forces and checkpoints left at least 53 people dead and more than 270 injured. Responsible for the attacks are Al Qaeda in Iraq and Iraqi Baath party. Islamic State of Iraq was responsible for the October 31 attack that attacked a Syrian Catholic church in Bagdad during Sunday evening Mass. At least 51 dead and 78 injured.

November 5- 2010, Pakistan another terrorist attack by Tehrik-i-Taliban Pakistan resulting the in the death of 66 people, including children, and wounding more than 80. The attack occurred in a mosque in the town of Darra Adam Khel, Khyber Pakhtunkhwa, Pakistan. People were wounded as worshippers offered Jumu'ah, the congregational Friday prayers. The bomber was targeting a local politician who was known for speaking out against the Taliban. December 7- 2010, India- the Islamist militant group, Indian Mujahideen, was responsible for another Terrorist Islamic bombing attack. 2 people died, a two-year-old girl was among the deaths, shed was killed sitting on her mother's lap, the mother was one of the three critically injured, more than 38 other people were injured. The blast occurred a day after the anniversary of the 1992 Badri Masjid demolition, in which a mosque was demolished at Ayodhya leading to nationwide religious riots killing over 2,000 people. The bombing happened in one of the holiest Hindu cities, Varanasi. The bomb was hidden inside a milk container on the Sheetla Ghat. An email by the Terrorist group, was sent to the media claiming responsibility for the attack. Later on the email was traced to WiFi connections in the Vashi suburb in Navi Mumbai by the Mumbai Police. The Indian Mujahideen claimed that claimed that had carried out the blast as a revenge for the supposedly "biased" Badri Masjid verdict of 30 September 2010. December 10-2010, Sweden- two bombs exploded in central Stockholm, killing the bomber (1) and injuring 2 other people. The perpetrator was an Iraqi-born Swedish citizen. The first bomb was a car explosion in an intersection in the city's downtown, the second one was of the bomber who blew himself up while wearing the explosives. It was described as the first suicide attack in the Nordic countries linked to Islamic terrorism. December 25, 2010- Pakistan- a female suicide bomber blows herself up in the middle of a crowd at a United Nations food center in the Bajaur region; 1 dead.

Year 2010 had seen 15 attacks; more than 623 people died from Islamic Terrorists attacks, and 1,684 wounded victims.

January 1- 2011, Egypt- 23 people died and 97 injured in an Islamic Terrorist attack on Coptic Christians in Alexandria, Egypt. While Christian worshipers were leaving a New Year service, an explosive device detonated in front of the Coptic Orthodox church of Saint Mark and Pope Peter in the Sidi Bishr neighborhood in Alexandria. It was a suicide bombing attack, perpetuated either by a Terrorist group called Army of Islam (the group however, quickly denied responsibility, while reportedly expressing support for the bombing), or the Egyptian Interior Mistry itself after the Coptic

Church started to question the interior ministry of its lack of transparency. In July 2011, nobody had yet been brought to trial and various reports claim that Habib Ibrahim Al Adly, Interior Minister, was himself involved in the bombings.

January 18 to 20, 2011, Iraq- more suicide bombings in Baqubah, Karbala and Tikrit perpetuated by Islamic Terrorist group Islamic State of Iraq which claimed the Tikrit attack. Al-Qaeda was also a suspected organization for such attacks in the Iraqi soil. At least 137 people died and more than 230 victims injured during the three days attacks. January 24- 2011, Russia- Domodedovo International Airport bombing was executed by Islamic fanatics, a fraction of the Caucasus Emirate and Riyad-us Saliheen Brigade terrorist group. The bombing killed 37 people died and 173 injured. The bombing affected the baggage-claim area of the airport's international arrivals hall. Some reports have suggested that the explosion was the caused by an improvised device packed with shrapnel, pieces of chopped wire and the equivalent to between two and five kilograms of TNT. January 27, February 12- 2011, Iraq- two bombing attacks, the first in Baghdad killing 48 and wounding 78 people, and the second in Samara responsible of the death of 48 and 80 people injured. Claim for both attacks go to Islamic Terrorist group Al-Qaeda in Iraq.

March 2- 2011, Germany- at the Frankfurt Airport, an Islamic fanatic (Arid Uka) opened fire in the back of the head of an American airman, killing him. Shouting "Allahu Akbar: the attacker then entered the same bus where other American airmen were waiting to be transported to a close by Air base, shooting and killing the driver, and continued to fire three shots at two other airmen, wounding them. When he pointed his pistol at the head of another airman and pulled the trigger, the weapon jammed. Uka fled, but was pursued by the civilian airport employee Lamar Joseph Conner and Staff Sergeant Trevor Donald Brewer and shortly afterwards overpowered by two German police officers. He was then arrested.

2 American citizens killed and 2 wounded. March 8, 2011- Pakistan-the Terrorist Islamic Tehrik-i-Taliban, referred to as Pakistani Taliban has been responsible for this 2011 Car explosive attack, occurred in the Pakistani city of Faisalabad, Punjab. At least 25 people died and over 127 victims injured when a car bomb blast occurred in a compressed natural gas station in Faisalabad. March 29, Iraq- 6 to 8 insurgents from the Islamic State of Iraq, gunmen wearing suicide belts hidden under military uniforms entered Tikrit, Iraq. The men presented themselves as Iraqi soldiers when they arrived at the security checkpoint. After being asked they needed to be searched, the open fired on the guards. They then blew up a car to create diversion by the council headquarters. The attacks were targeting politicians, citizens and journalists. The death toll reached 65 dead and around 100 wounded people. The Islamic State of Iraq ceased to exist in April 2013, then transformed itself into Islamic State of Iraq and Levant (ISIL, ISIS Islamic State of Iraq and Syria, IS), which is still active today (2016). Jordanian Abu Musab al-Zarqawi, a 1966 born veteran of the Soviet war in Afghanistan (1979-`989), in 1999 he started a militant group called Jama'at al-Tawhid wal-Jihad (Organization of Monotheism and Jihad) aiming to overthrow the 'apostate' kingdom of Jordan. In October 2004, Zarqawi pledged alliance to Osama bin Laden and changed the name of his group to Tanzim Qaidat al-Jihad fi Bilad al-Rafidayn (Organization of Jihad's Base in Mesopotamia), often referred to Al Qaeda in Iraq. That only shows that most of the Islamic Terrorists groups were radically either created or changed their visions after the Afghan-Soviet war, or also, were a creation to go after and try to attack and destroy their own rulers, governments, or even their own people. That's what actually lead to, and explain the happening of the Arab Spring, people took action in their hands for the same purpose those organization couldn't accomplish. Those terrorist organizations were created from people, and civilians that were upset with the system, and they were built to do a change of power.

May 5- 2011, Iraq- same Terrorist Organization, Islamic State of Iraq (ISI), claimed the lives of 24 people and injuring more than 72, in a suicide bombing aimed to Iraqi Police, in the city of Al Hillal. A suicide bomber detonated a car full of explosives at a local police station. A few days after the explosion the ISI claimed responsibility for it, saying it was a revenge for the death of Osama Bin Laden on 2 May 2011. Osama Bin Laden (March 10, 1957 – May 2, 2011) was the founder of al-Qaeda, the organization that claimed the responsibility for the September 11, 2001 attacks on the United States, along with numerous other mass-casualty attacks against civilian and military targets. He was a Saudi Arabian, a member of the wealthy bin Laden family, and an ethnic Yemeni Kindite. Kindah is the name of an Arab kingdom by the Kindah tribe, the tribe's existence dates to the second century BCE (before the Common Era). Bin Laden was born to the family of billionaire Mohammed bin Awad bin Laden in Saudi Arabia. He studied at university in the Saudi Arabia until 1979, when he joined Mujahideen forces in Pakistan fighting against the Soviet Union in Afghanistan. He helped to fund Mujahideen by providing arms, money and fighters from the Arab world into Afghanistan, and gained popularity among many Arabs. In the years 1990s' he hired many followers from the Arab world and North Africa to go and fight in Afghanistan, which created the doctrine of fighting for Islam, and therefore, started the new era of fighting westerners. In 1988, he formed al-Qaeda. He was banished from Saudi Arabia in 1992 (which explain again how Islamic terrorist were first targeting the main power governments in their own countries), and shifted his base to Sudan, until U.S. pressure forced him to leave Sudan in 1996. After establishing a new base in Afghanistan, he declared a war against the United States of America, initiating a series of bombings and related attacks. The FBI placed a $25 million bounty on him, he was a major target of the War on terror. On May 2, 2011, bin Laden was shot and killed inside a private residential compound in Abbottabad, where he lived with a local family from Waziristan, during a covert operation conducted by members of the United States naval Special Warfare Development Group and Central Intelligence Agency operators on the orders of U.S. president Barack Obama.

May 7, 2011, Egypt- the 2011 Imbaba church attacks were a series of attacks that took place on 7 may 2011 against Coptic Christian churches in the poor working-class neighborhood of Imbaba in cairo, Egypt. The attacks were blamed on Salafi Muslims, and claimed the deaths of 15 people and injured more than 232 victims. The attacks began when a mob of estimated 500 Salafi Muslims attacked the church of Saint Mina, claiming that a Christian convert to Islam was held hostage there. Christians denied that anybody was being held hostage, and police search of the church did not reveal anything. Yet, Salafi Muslims insisted on attacking the church, and opened gunfire at Christians who refused that the Muslims raid the church. They opened gunfire, and threw firebombs and Molotov cocktails. After destroying the Coptic church of Saint Mina, Salafis went ahead and burned another church, the Coptic Orthodox church of the Virgin Mary, also in Imbaba. July 7, 2011, China- Hotan, Xinjang, China, was the place of an Islamic terrorist attack with a bomb and knife assault, which killed 18 and injured 4 people. It was an invasion of police station and a hostage crisis. A group of 18 young Uyghur men, an Islamic terrorist and separatist organization founded by Uyghur militants in western China, with the goal of the independence of East Turkestan from China, who opposed the local government's campaign against the full-face Islamic veil perpetrated a series of coordinated bomb and knife attacks and occupied a police station on Nuerbage street, killing two security guards and taking eight hostages. The attackers yelled religious slogans, including ones associated with Jihadism. July 30, 2011, China- another attack by Uyghur men. They hijacked a truck, killed its driver and drove into a crowd of pedestrians. The attacks involved a series of knife and bomb attacks, occurred in Kashgar, China. They then got out of the vehicle and attacked pedestrians with knives. On July 31, a chain of two explosives started a fire in a restaurant, killing 15 people and injuring 42. September 7, 2011, India- with the time, it became more usual to find just extremist terrorist that don't belong to any organization doing Islamic Terrorist attacks for personal motives, and claiming Jihad for God, and later on, reporting that they had allegiance to some fanatic groups. This attack was an example of few Muslim extremist that killed 17 people and wounded 76 innocent people, in the Indian capital Delhi. It was a bombing, with explosives been placed in a briefcase at the high court reception where hundreds of people throng every day to attend court cases. Responsibility for the blast was claimed by Harkat-el-Jihad al-Islami. October 4, 2011, Somalia- Al-Shabaab Islamic Terrorist group was responsible for the killing of 100 people and wounding more than 110 people, in an attack when a suicide bomber drove a truck into the gate of the Transitional Federal Government's ministerial complex in Mogadishu, Somalia. They claimed responsibility for the attack. It is a very active Terrorist Islamic group operating from 2006 till present. A Jihadist terrorist militant group based in East Africa. In 2012, it pledged allegiance to the militant Islamist organization Al-Qaeda. According to several reports the attack was aimed at 150 young Somalis who were to be flown to Sudan to be trained as spies, but instead resulted in the death of mostly students and parents awaiting news about scholarships to Sudan and Turkey from the Ministry of Higher Education.

October 7-13, 2011, Iraq- Islamic State of Iraq was responsible for a series of bombing attacks that hit the capital of Iraq, Bagdad, between the 7 and the 13 of October 2011. Targets were civilian population and Iraqi police, with various shootings, suicide bombings and car bombs, resulted in the death of 64 people and 190 injuries. October 28, 2011, Bosnia and Herzegovina- Wahhabism is a religious movement or brunch of Sunni Islam. It has been described as orthodox and fundamentalist. On that day, a

Wahhabi Islamist attacked the US embassy in Sarajevo, the capital and largest city of Bosnia and Herzegovina, with firearm. He wounded a police officer before being shot and injured by police. December 22, 2001, Iraq- Islamic State of Iraq perpetuated a series of coordinated attacks, in Bagdad, targeting civilians and government offices, with suicide bombings, suicide car bombing, roadside bombs, shootings and sticky bombs (bombs that are type anti-tank hand grenades). This was the first major attack following U.S. withdrawal from Iraq, and, resulted in the death of 60 to 72 people, with 160 to 217 injured victims. The Islamic State of Iraq claimed the attacks were the latest in what they described as a series of special invasions to support the weak Sunnis in the prisons of the apostates and to retaliate for the captives who were executed by the Safavid government. The term Safavid makes reference to the Persian or Iranian, it actually refers to the government of Prime Minister Nouri al Maliki, a Shia politician who is accused by the Islamic State of Iraq of being under Iran's sphere of influence. Malaki, immediately after the US withdrawal of its troop this month, has actually cracked down on Sunni politicians.

December 25, 2011, Nigeria- Boko Haram, is a Terrorist Islamic group, operating from 2002 till present, was responsible for 2011 series of bombings that occurred on Christmas Day. They were series of bomb blasts and shootings at churches in Madalla, Jos, Gadaka and Damuturu. More than 41 people died and more than 57 reported injured. Boko Haram, is a Muslim sect in Nigeria, it's an Islamic State of West Africa Province that pledged its support and allegiance to the ISIS, and changed its logo to the ISIS one, the Black Standard flag by ISIS, which was adopted by Boko Haram in 2015. Since the current insurgency started in 2009, the Islamic extremist group of Boko Haram, has killed 20,000 and displaced 2.3 million from their homes, from 2009 till 2015. It was founded as a Sunni Islamic fundamentalist sect, influenced by the Wahhabi movement, advocating a strict form of Sharia law. It developed into a Salafijihadi group in 2009, the year that led to a violent uprisings due to Boko Haram's increasing radicalization in the country. Same year, their leader was executed. That was accompanied by increasingly sophisticated attacks and progressing in 2011 to include suicide bombings of police buildings and the United Nations office in Abuja. In 2012 a state of emergency was declared to cover the entire northeast of Nigeria. Corruption in the security services and human rights abuses committed by them have hampered efforts to counter the unrest. The name of Boko Haram is usually translated to "Western education is forbidden". Haram is from the Arabic, means forbidden, and the Hausa word of Boko means fake. Hausa is the Chadic language (a branch of the Afro-asiatic language family) with the largest number of speakers, spoken as first language by about 35 million people, and the second language by 15 million in Nigeria, and millions more in other countries, for a total of at least 50 million speakers.

December 28, 2011, China- a group of 15 Uyghur youths crossing the border into Pakistan for jihadist training kidnapped two goat shepherds for directions. They were soon confronted by police to release the hostages. The group attacked the policemen with knives, killing one and injuring another. The police shot back, killing seven hostage takers, wounding and capturing four, and freeing the two shepherds. 8 dead and 5 injuries was the toll of such Islamic hostage situation.

2011 was a year mostly dominated by attacks realized by ISI (Islamic State of Iraq) around Bagdad and other cities controlled by new government, after the US withdrawal. The toll was of 19 Islamic Terrorist attacks, with more than 741 deaths and more than 1836 people injured.

January 5, 2012, Iraq- another attack by Islamic State of Iraq, targeting Shia civilians, resulted in the death of 73 people and injuring more than 149 people. They were series of attacks that hit the capital Baghdad and the southern city of Nasiriyah and appeared to target Shia Muslims. A suicide bomber attacked a security checkpoint as huge crowds of pilgrims were making their journey from Nasiriyah to Kerbala for a religious holiday. February 14, 2012, Thailand- bombings attempts by Iranian nationals to assassinate Israeli diplomats was an attempt that resulted in 5 people injured, in Bangkok, Thailand. February, 23, 2012, Iraq- more Iraqi attacks perpetuated by terrorist Islamic State of Iraq, resulting in the death of 83 people and more than 250 people injured. The attacks were the fifth simultaneous wave of bombings to hit Iraq during the insurgency and the second such major assault since the US withdrawal at the end of 2011. The umbrella group Islamic State of Iraq claimed responsibility for the bombings two days later and promised further bloodshed as it targets Shiites across Iraq. March 20, 2012, Iraq- another attack by Islamic State of Iraq (ISI) in Baghdad and at least 9 other cities, resulted in the death of 52 and more than 250 people injured. Attacks targeting Security offices and civilians (mostly Shiite), were in the form of suicide bombings, car bomb, IEDs and shootings. March 20, 2012, France- the Toulouse and Montauban shootings were a series of three gun attacks targeting French soldiers and Jewish civilians. The motive of the perpetrator, an Islamic fanatic, were antisemitism and extremist Islamic beliefs. In total, he killed 7, plus himself, and injuring 5 others. The perpetrator was identified as Mohammed Merah, a 23 year old French, of Algerian descent. The police investigation suggested that he was not working alone and had made more than 1,800 calls to over 180 contacts in 20 different countries, in addition to several trips to the Middle East and Afghanistan. Merah admitted anti-Semitic motivations, and said he attacked the Jewish school because "the Jews kill our brothers and sisters in Palestine".

May 3, 2012, Russia- the 2012 Makhachkala attack occurred on 3 May 2012 after two suicide bombers detonated explosive-filled cars near a traffic police checkpoint in Makhachkala, a city in the republic of Dagestan, Russia, killing at least 13 people and wounding more than 130 victims. The Salafist Jihadist organization of Chechen, The Caucasus Emirate, mostly active from 2007 till present in southwestern Russia and Syria, was responsible for the blast.

May 21, 2012, Yemen- a bombing suicide attack has been perpetrated by an Islamic Jihadist group, calling itself, Ansar al-Sharia. Ansar al-Sharia, or Jama'at Ansar al'Shari'a, is a Yemen-based umbrella organization which includes units from several Islamic groups, including al-Qaeda in the Arabian Peninsula. It was created on 2011, and still operating today. On October 2012, the United States Department of State amended its list of Foreign Terrorist Organizations to designate Ansar al-Sharia in Yemen as an alias for al-Qaeda in the Arabians Peninsula, rather than listing it as a separate organization. The suicide bombing was against Yemeni Army soldiers practicing for the annual Unity Day military in Sana'a, Yemen. A day, (May 22) that mark the unification of North Yemen and South Yemen as the Republic of Yemen. The suicide bombing came 10 days into an army offensive against al-Qaeda in Yemen's restive southern Abyan province, where the Al-Qaeda in the Arabian Peninsula have seized control of a string of towns and cities in attacks launched since 2011. The attack was a retaliation, and took place in al-Sabin Square, near Yemen's presidential palace, as soldiers were arranging themselves in a parade rehearsal for the upcoming Unity Day ceremonies. More than 120 people died in this Jihadist Islamic attack, with close to 350 injured.

June 13, 2012- Iraq- reports stimulated the involvement of the Islamic State of Iraq in a series of simultaneous bombings and shootings occurred in different cities in Iraq, as the attacks mostly appeared to target Shi'ite pilgrims. Pilgrims were gathered to commemorate the death of imam Moussa al-Kadhim. At least 93 people were killed and over 300 wounded in such coordinated attacks across Iraq. Locations targeted by the Islamic Terrorist attacks were Baghdad, Kirkuk, Taj, Hila, Mosul, Karbala and Balad. June 29- 2012, China- Tianjin Airlines Flight 7554 was a scheduled passenger flight, that day of June 29, between Hotan and Urumqi in China's Xinjiang Autonomous Region. Within ten minutes after taking off, six ethnic Uyghur men, one of whom allegedly professed his motivation as Jihad, announced their intent to hijack the aircraft, according to multiple witnesses. Passengers and crew resisted and successfully stopped the hijackers. The aircraft turned and returned to Holan, where 11 passengers and crew and two hijackers were treated for injuries. Two (2) hijackers died from severe injuries during the fight on board. The attack was the first attempted hijacking attack since 9/11 attack in USA.

July 18, 2012, Bulgaria- Hezbollah and Iran were the main suspect of the terrorist attack carried out by a suicide bomber on a passenger bus transporting Israeli tourists at the Burgas Airport in Burgas, Bulgaria on July 18, 2012. The bus was carrying 42 Israelis from the airport to their hotels, after arriving on flight from Tel Aviv. The explosion killed 6 people; the Bulgarian bus driver and five Israelis and injured 32 Israelis. Iran has been playing the role of bad influence for many years, many centuries. This country has been using Islam as backdoor, and justification for all its malicious, and "evil" behavior. This country has been in an ongoing indirect conflict with Israel. Its government has not recognized Israel as a state, referring to its government as the "Zionist regime". The conflict is bound in the political struggle of Iranian leadership against Israel, that have been fueled by the Palestinian conflict, and the counter aim of Israel to prevent alleged nuclear weapons from the Iranian government and downgrading its allies and proxies such Hezbollah party in Lebanon. Iranian forces are operating in Syria in huge support of Bashar al-Assad's government. Iran is in a strong process of establishing a surface of influence throughout Iraq, Syria, Lebanon, Yemen and parts of Central Asia. Israel believe that after Assad, Iran will establish a strong presence in the region, and they are going to move and defect their effort and attack Israel. Iran, in the same prospect, in contact with the U.S. over the fight against ISIS (Islamic State of Iraq and Syria) has said that Israel would be at risk if the U.S. and its coalition sought to topple Assad.

July 23, August 16 and September 9, 2012, Iraq- three dates with major attacks perpetrated by ISI (Islamic State of Iraq). Car bombs, suicide bombings and shootings took the lives of 116 people and injured about 300 people in the July 23 attacks. They were targeting Security forces, government buildings and Shia Muslim neighborhoods. The following attacks were taken at across central and northern Iraq, killing 128 and sounding 417 innocent people. Including roadside bombs, and targeting Iraqi security forces and Shia civilians. On the September 9, same targets resulted in the deaths of more than 108 people from Iraqi security forces and Shiite civilians, and injuring more than 371 people.

September 11, 2012, Libya-U.S. - "2012 Benghazi" attack on the U.S. Consulate, by Islamic Jihadist groups Ansar al-Sharia, Al-Qaeda in the Islamic Maghreb, Al Qaeda in Iraq, Al-Qaeda in the Arabian Peninsula and Omar Abdul Rahman Brigades were al responsible for the killing of four (4) U.S. citizens, including US ambassador J. Christopher Stevens. The attacks resulted in the death of about 100 Libyan attackers. Such Terrorist Islamic attacks were well-coordinated, with armed assault, rioting, arson, using rocket-propelled grenades, hand grenades, assault rifles, guns, truck mounted artillery, diesel canisters and mortars. On that evening of September 11, 2012, Islamic militants attacked the American diplomatic compound in the city of Benghazi, Libya. There was a second attack, hours later, targeted a different compound about one mile away, killing two (2) CIA contractors, and injuring ten (10) others.

2012 was marked by the increasing influence of Jihadist attacks against sites in Iraq by ISI, and ended the year by the hatred

Islamic Barbarian Jihadist riots that resulted in the Benghazi attacks. The toll was of 14 Islamic attacks, with the death of more than 888 people, and 2203 injured.

January 10- 2013, Pakistan- the attacks organized against Shia Muslims living in Pakistan didn't stop, and this one is an example of how barbarian the Jihadists can be. Several bombings took place in the southwestern Pakistani city of Quetta, the capital of Balochistan Province, killing at least a total of 130 people and injuring more than 270. The terrorist group Lashkar-e-Jhangvi was responsible for the attacks, an Islamic Jihadist organization that been operating from 1996 till now. January 16, 2013- Algeria- Militants from a terrorist group calling itself Al-Mourabitoun jihadists, took hostages from different nationalities, and demanded an end to the French military operations against Islamists in northern Mali, in return for the safety of the hostages. The group was an affiliated to al-Qaeda. The terrorists had guns on them, and threating the hostages to kill them; they affixed bombs to some of the captives. The crisis began when around 32 Islamist terrorists in 4 to 5 vehicles, entered Algeria from Libya and northern Mali, attacked a bus transporting employees from a natural gas plant near the town of the border with Libya, killing a number of the employees. The main motive for those Islamic attacks was to oppose "operation Serval", an operation where French military trying to oust Islamic militants in the north of Mali, who had begun a push into the center of Mali. The hostage situation led to the death of at least 67 people. The brigade that made the attack was led by Mokhtar Belmokhtar, a terrorist escaping from Mali after the French attacks on his country. One of his senior lieutenants, Abdul al Nigeri, led the attack and was among the terrorists killed. Al-Mourabitoun is composed mostly of Tuaregs and Arabs from the northern Mali regions of Timbuktu, Kidal and Gao, but also includes Algerians, Tunisians and other nationalities. It was created in 2013, is an African militant jihadist organization formed between Ahmed

Ould Amer, a.k.a. Ahmed al-Tilmsi's Movement for Oneness and Jihad in West Africa and Mokhtar Belmokhtar's Masked Men Brigade. It is a branch of the al-Qaeda in the Islamic Maghreb organization (AQIM). A total of 685 Algerian workers and 107 foreigners were freed, but more than 69 died from the attacks of Amenas hostage crisis.

February 16- 2013, Pakistan- another Terrorist Islamic attack on Quetta (this time the city's outskirt), the capital city of Balochistan, Pakistan. The bomb, hidden in a water tank, exploded at a market in Hazara Town, killing at least 110 people and injuring more than 200 victims. The Lashkar-e-Jhangvi group claimed responsibility for the blast, the second attack against the Shia Hazaras in a month. Acts of violence involving Sunni Muslims and their Shia counterparts in Pakistan have been evident since the 1980s. February 21- 2013, India- two blasts occurred in the city of Hyderabad, India. The death toll was of 17 people and injuring more than 119 people. The bombs exploded in a crowded shopping area, targeting civilians. Indian Mujahideen, a Terrorist organization, created in 2008 and still operating, was responsible for the blasts. It is a terrorist group that has carried out several attacks against civilians targets in India. In June 2010, it was declared as a terrorist organization and banned by the Government of India. In September 2011, the US officially placed the Indian Mujahideen on its list of foreign terrorist organizations, with the State Department acknowledging that the group had engaged in several terrorist attacks in India and had aspirations with the ultimate aim of creating an "Islamic caliphate" across South Asia.

March 19- 2013, Iraq- militias from the terrorist organization ISI attacked Shia civilians and Iraqi Police Forces in one of its latest operations before it joined and combined the group to be called ISIS (Islamic State of Iraq and Syria). In these attacks across Iraq, in one day, they killed at least 98 and wounded a minimum of 240 people. The attacks consist in car bombings, suicide bombings, roadside bombings and shootings. The attacks coincided with the tenth anniversary of the beginning of the Iraq War.

April 15, 2013, United States of America- Boston Marathon Bombings. It was a terrorist attack, planned by two Chechen Muslim Terrorist brothers, Dzhokhar Tsarnaev and Tamerlan Tsarnaev, to kill innocent people at the finish line of the Boston Marathon, Massachusetts, US. The two Jihadists exploded a two pressure cooker bombs, with a 12 second and 190m apart. They escaped from the scene, and an unprecedented manhunt for both of them ensued later on, with thousands of law enforcement officers searching for them. The bombs killed 3 civilians on April 15, and injured a 264 estimated number of civilians. During the manhunt, on 18 April, 1 police officer was shot to death, then on April 19, another police officer was injured in an explosion and then died the year after from the injuries, and 16 other police officers were wounded during the gunfight of the same day. Total deaths for the attacks were 6, and 280 injured. Islamic beliefs was the number one motive the brothers' terrorists acts. May 11, 2013, Turkey- two car bombs exploded in the town of Reyhanli, Hayat Province, Turkey, 5 km from the Syrian border. It resulted for the death of 52 and 140 people injured. Many Syrian refugees have passed through the town while fleeing from the civil war in their own country. While some Syrians refugees were caught in the blasts, the majority of fatalities involved were local Turks, and some residents blamed the Turkish government for bringing the war in Syria to the town. Responsibility for the attacks was never claimed by any group, and the suspected for those operations were either ISIS, "al-Qaeda elements", Syrian government or Mukhabarat, Acilciler, Al-Nusra Front or even some suggested were Turks with ties to pro-government Syrian groups. Mukhabarat is the Military Intelligence service and armed organization of the Syrian Government, they operate under Syrian President "Al-Assad). Turkish authorities suspected that a former Turkish Marxist group Acilciler, with ties to the Syrian military intelligence service Mukhabarat, might have ordered the attacks. Al-Nusra group is a Sunni Islamist militia terrorist Jihadist group, fighting against Syrian Government forces in the Syrian Civil War, with the aim of establishing an Islamist state in the country. It is the Syrian branch of Al-Qaeda in the Levant or in Syria. It also operate in Lebanon. However, the Islamic State of Iraq and the Levant (ISIS or ISIL) was formerly part of al-Qaeda, but was disavowed by al-Qaeda General Command, which stated: "it is not affiliated with al-Qaeda and has no relationship with it… al-Qaeda is not responsible for ISIS's actions" BBC.com, February 3, 2014 (Al-Qaeda has insisted it has no links with the Islamic State in Iraq and the Levant (ISIS), which has been locked in deadly clashes with rebels in Syria. An online statement purportedly from the group's general command said ISIS was "not a branch of al-Qaeda").

May 22, 2013, England- Lee James Rigby, was a 25-year-old British Army soldier, a drummer and machine-gunner in the 2nd Battalion of the Royal Regiment of Fusiliers. He had a two-year-old son at the time of his death, and was engaged to his new fiancée. While Rigby was crossing the road to get to a shop, two men, were later identified as Michael Olumide Adebolajo and Michael Oluwatobi Adebowale, two British of Nigerian descent. They drove a car at him at 30 to 40 miles per hour, knocking him to the ground. They then attacked him with knives and a cleaver, trying to behead him. The killers remained at the scene and asked bystanders to call the police. Immediately after the attack, some passers-by stood over Rigby's body to protect him from further injury. While awaiting for the police, the assailants were saying they were responsible for killing the man on the ground because he "killed Muslims in Iraq and in Afghanistan". In a video shot by a bystander, Adebolajo said: "the only reason we killed this man today is because Muslims are dying by British soldiers. And this British soldier is one … By Allah, we swear by the almighty Allah we will never stop fighting you until you leave us alone". The attacks were a retaliation for the British military's presence in Islamic countries. After the police arrived, the two men had a revolver and knives pointed at the police. Armed police fired eight times and both men wounded then arrested.

Allah doesn't exist, period. And even if it does, people don't have the right to kill others under such circumstances like Rigby's case. Therefore, it was a criminal terrorist act, by two criminal terrorist minds.

May 23, 2013- Niger- MUJAO is an active Jihadist Terrorist militant organization that broke off from al-Qaeda in the Islamic Maghreb. It was created on 2011, with the goal to extend its Jihadist propaganda across West Africa. However its operations have been limited to southern Algeria and northern Mali. On May 23 2013, two coordinated attacks took places in two Niger towns of Agadez and Arlit. The targets were Niger and French citizens for their supports to stop killing innocent people under the use of "so called" the Religion of Islam. These Islamist affiliates' attacks resulted in the death of 26 people and wounded more than 30 others. MUJAO later claimed responsibility saying: "We attacked France and Niger (for its cooperation with France) in the war against sharia (Islamic law)".

The exact definition and explanation of what MUJAO do or any other Islamic entity to justify the killing of any one person is: A Barbarian act (or acts) by ignorant people using Religion (Islam in this case) to kill and terrorize other human beings. The justification is always the same: Jihad for god's will. A justification that has nothing to do with a clean healthy mind; these terrorists are brainwashed from head to toe. Everything these Terrorists do is a mistake, a lie and injustice to mankind.

May 23, 2013, France- a Christian French, Alexandre Dhaussy, correction: a recent Christian convert to Islam, was the Terrorist attacker to a French soldier named Cedric Cordier. He stabbed him in the Paris suburb of La Defense in what has been described as a terrorist attack. Weeks before the incident, due to the France involvement and campaign to liberate northern Mali from Islamist occupation, France was on high alert to a threat from al-Qaeda in North Africa. Some 450 soldiers were placed on patrol in train stations and other locations in Paris. Cedric Cordier was one of the soldiers to be deployed there. He was attacked in the afternoon of that day by a man with knife. The attacker stabbed him in the neck and fled into a crowded shopping area. He was arrested next day, and admitted the attack to the police who arrested him. Dhaussy, unemployed and homeless, refused many times to work with women, once the police stopped him when he acted suspicious as he didn't want to wait for a bus with women. He repeatedly invoked the name of Allah during his detention.

The Religion of Islam doesn't give the same right to women as men. It is a prejudicial religion that needs either to adapt or to be banned. Lot of examples show how inequality exist between genders, and prove just how wrong Islam's religion is. In the matter related to Heritage –under Islamic Law- after someone's death, Islam's Law gives the man double the wealth of what the woman gets. In juridical procedure, when a person is needed to testify in a court, the man's testimonial equals two women words. Those are only two examples of how inequality between women and men existed for centuries in the Muslim world. It is not fair that we are in the 21st century and governments, Presidents or Kings in the Muslim countries still abiding and enforcing such inequality in the gender matter. Sometimes, in many cases, Kings in the Arab Muslim countries have to make sure they don't get girls as their first-born. Moroccan King's dynasty is an example of how cruel can it get if the first born would be a girl, and who knows what they do with a first-born girl? Does a King, himself or his entourage, make them girls (first-born) disappear? The smartest way, and that's what actually they do, is not to give them the right to be Queens; the Law states only first male-born can be in charge, and if it's a girl, well let's hope for the opposite gender to be next.

May 27, 2013, Iraq- from a number of 3,000 deaths per month during the years 2006-07, violence in Iraq decreased significantly then to rise again in 2012. Starting 2012, Sunnis began protesting against the Shia-led government. The protests had been largely peaceful, but then affected by the war in neighboring Syria, the attacks started to take significant violence on them. On 27 May 2013, a series of coordinated attacks occurred in Baghdad, the capital of Iraq, killing 71 people and injuring more than 224 others. The Islamic State of Iraq, ISI was the group responsible for the attacks. Almost all the attacks in the capital took place at marketplaces or in crowded shopping areas of Shi'ite districts. June 15, 2013, Pakistan- terrorist Islamic attacks by the group Lashkar-e-Jhangvi has been occurring more often in Pakistan, targeting the Shi'ite population. Two bombing devices have resulted in the death of 26 and injured more than 20 people. The first attack was deployed against a bus carrying female students, killing 14 of them and injuring 19 others. A short time later, another blast, this time at a nearby Medical center, that was actually treating the victims from the first attack, resulted in more damages. Later on a Quetta political officials visiting the injured were attacked by a team of five gunmen, sparking hours of shootout with security forces, resulting in at least 12 casualties. It is believed that the attacks were intended to be targeting Shia from Hazara ethnic minority, however, due to an earlier change of route, the bus carried a more ethnically mixed group of people, and has been described as the wrong target by the perpetrators. Balochistan, and its minority ethnic in Hazara, have been a target place for many of those terrorist Islamic attacks because of the Shia's Muslims presence. June 22, 2013, Pakistan- ten (10) tourists' climbers were killed by 16 Taliban and al-Qaeda attackers. The terrorists entered the base camp, at the mountain, where they were trying to climb the ninth highest mountain in the world. The site of the attack is located 4,200 meters above sea-level and can only be approached via foot or horseback. The attackers gained access to this location by abducting two Pakistani guides. One of the climbers' survivors described what the attackers were shouting "they were shouting God is Great, long live Islam and long live Osama bin laden ... this is revenge for Sheikh bin Laden". Who cares about Bin Laden? Only desperate people, people with no values. The main motive for the attack was a sort of retaliation against the U.S. drone strike on Pakistan territory. The Terrorist Islamic group, Tehrik-i-Taliban Pakistan, claimed responsibility for the attack. The group's spokesperson said "through this killing we gave a message to international community to ask U.S. to stop drone strike". The tourists that died were from: one was an American with dual Chinese citizenship; three came from Ukraine, two from Slovakia, one other from China and one from Lithuania; one a Sherpa from Nepal.

July 7, 2013, India- the Islamic Terrorist group Indian Mujahideen, operating from 2008 till present, was responsible the bombings of areas in and around the Mahabodhi Temple complex, a UNESCO World Heritage Site in Bodh Gaya, India. Five (5) people were injured, including two Buddhist monks.

September 13, 2013, Afghanistan- the U.S. consulate in Herat, Afghanistan was attacked on this day by a group of Taliban militants, killing 8 guards, 8 attackers and 1 Afghan officer. Total dead 17 people and 20 injured. September 21, 2013, Kenya- the extremist Islamic Terrorist group al-Shabaab claimed responsibility for the incident that resulted in the death of 67 people, including 4 attackers, and more than 175 people wounded in the mass shooting terrorist attack to the Westgate shopping mall, the most upscale mall in Nairobi, Kenya. Al-Shabaab, is a jihadist terrorist group based in East Africa, operating from 2006 till present. Its troop strength was estimated at 7,000 to 9,000 militants in 2014, it pledged alliance to al-Qaeda in 2012. As of 2015, the group retreated from the major cities, controlling a few rural areas. The group describes itself as waging Jihad against "enemies of Islam", and is engaged in combat against the Federal Government of Somalia and the African Union Mission to Somalia. September 22, 2013, Pakistan- on this day, a twin suicide bomb attack took place at All Saints Church in Peshawar, Pakistan, in which 127 people were killed and over 250 injured. It was the deadliest attack on the Christian minority in the history of Pakistan. The Tehrik-i-Taliban Pakistan-linked group Jundallah claimed responsibility for the attack, they said that the attack on Christians and non-Muslims will not stop until US drone attacks in Pakistan cease. Jundallah militant group also vowed allegiance, in November 2014, to the Islamic State of Iraq and the Levant (ISIS). More alliance for evil.

September 29, 2013, Nigeria- gunmen from Boko Haram, the terrorist Islamic group, entered a male dormitory in the College of Agriculture in Gujba, Yobe State, Nigeria, killing 44 students and teachers. They opened fire on the students while they were asleep. Only the male sleeping quarters were targeted.

Boko Haram was founded in 2002 to fight against the de-Arabization of Nigeria, which the group maintains is the root cause of criminal behavior in the country. From 2009 to 2013, violence linked to the terrorist group resulted in 3,600 deaths, including 1,600 civilians. Since 2010, Boko Haram has targeted schools, killing hundreds of students.

October 28, 2013, China- a car crashed outside of the Gate of Heavenly Peace on Tiananmen Square, Beijing, in what police described as a terrorist suicide attack. Five (5) people died in the incident and 38 injured. The motive of the attack were related to be fueled by Extremist Islamic Beliefs.

Turkistan Islamic Party, operating from 1997 till present, is an Islamic terrorist and separatist organization founded by Uyghur militants in western China. Its desirable goals are the independence of East Turkestan from China, the establishment of an Islamic state across the entire Central Asia and a caliphate. All of the terrorists groups want power; that's most of what they looking for: a State, a Caliphate. They striving for power, using religion as a bait for followers.

December 5, 2013, Yemen- the attack started when few gunmen killed four guards surrounding the ministry compound. After the gate was open, a suicide bomber drove an explosive-laden car into the western entrance of the Defense Ministry complex. Next day, Ansar al-Sharia, a militant Islamic group linked to al-Qaeda has claimed responsibility for the attack that killed 56 and wounded more than 200 people. Yemeni military investigators say 12 militants, mostly Saudi nationals, were responsible for the attack. Jama'at Ansar al-Shari'a, also known as Ansar al-Sharia, is a Yemen-based terrorist Islamic umbrella organization which includes units from several militant Islamic groups, including al-Qaeda in the Arabian Peninsula. Among the victim death's toll on December's attack were, 20 were from Yemen, 7 from Philippines, 2 Germans, 2 Vietnamese, and 1 Indian.

2013 has seen a total of 20 Islamic known Jihadist attacks. The toll was 932 dead, with 2,079 wounded.

January 19, 2014, Pakistan- Taliban kept on retaliating against the drones the U.S. employed on its strikes in Pakistan. This time, it was a bombing attack by the Taliban that killed 26 Pakistani soldiers, and injured more than 38 others. The bomb was placed in a van, and exploded at an army checkpoint. February 14, 2014, Nigeria- another massacre by the Islamist group Boko Haram against Christian Villagers in Borno State, Nigeria. Dressed in military gear, dozens of Islamist militants raided the predominantly Christian village, shooting at some civilians with guns, and killing others with knives in a throat slit manner. By the end of next day,

February 15, at least 121 people have been killed. Militants yelling the phrase "Allah Akbar" while attacking the village. The following day, Boko Haram launched a similar style attack, killing over 90 Christians in Gwosa, Nigeria. The terrorists proceeded then to attack the Nigerian Army, killing 9 Nigerian soldiers. Total of deaths, at least, 220 people.

March 1, 2014, China- at the evening of that first day of May, 2014, a group of individuals dressed on black clothes, rushed into the square lobby of Kunming Railway Station and started to attack people indiscriminately. Both male and female attackers pulled out long-bladed knives and slashed and stabbed passengers. The terrorists killed 29 people and injured 143. Though no group or individual has claimed responsibility, East Turkestan Islamic Movement was blamed for the attacks. However, no direct blame was expressed by any source. Because no blame was directed to by any news media, after the attacks, people were angry at how the coverage was presented to the public, and blame the media for not labelling the acts at "terrorist attacks". April 14, 2014, Nigeria- Boko Haram was created on 2002, is a group of people of Sunnah for Preaching and Jihad, they seek the establishment of an Islamic state in Nigeria, period. They oppose the Westernization of Nigerian society and the concentration of the wealth of the country among members of a small political elite, mainly in the Christian south of the country. For that reason, they are killing thousands and thousands of innocent people. On April 2014, two bombs exploded at a crowded bus station in Nyanya, Nasarawa, Nigeria. The bombs, some hidden inside vehicles detonated during morning rush hour, killed more than 88 people and injuring more than 200. Boko Haram claimed responsibility for the bombing six days after it occurred.

April 30, 2014, China- Turkestan Islamic Party was claimed for this terrorist attack that coincided with the last day visit of Xi Jinping, General Secretary of the Communist Party of China to

Xinjiang. A knife attack and bombing occurred in the Chinese city of Urumqi, Xinjiang. Two assailants attacked passengers and detonated explosives at the Urumqi railway station. The attack, left three (3) people dead and seventy-nine (79) others wounded. It is not known if Xi was still in the province when the attack took place. On the morning of the attack, he visited a mosque and urged religious leaders to forge a better understanding of the religious teachings.

May 20, 2014, Nigeria- in 2012, multiple churches were bombed by Boko Haram in order to try to start a religious conflict between Christians and Muslims. On April 15, same year, Boko Haram abducted over 200 schoolgirls, kidnapped from the Government Secondary School in the town of Chibok in Borno State, Nigeria. Thousands of people have been killed in attacks perpetrated by the Terrorist group of Boko Haram, and the Nigerian federal government declared a state of emergency in May 2013 in Borno State in its fight against the insurgency. On May 2014, two bombs exploded in Jos, Plateau State, Nigeria, killing at least 118 people and injuring more than 56 others. Two bombs; the first occurred 30 minutes before the second goes, the first explosion occurred in the Terminus Market; the second explosion took place near a hospital. The second explosion killed potential rescuers who had gone to assist after the first bomb exploded.

May 22, 2014, China- Urumqi, the capital of China's Xinjiang Ughur Autonomous Region's was the theater of an assault by terrorist attacks. A two SUVs which carried five assailants, were driven into a street market in Urumqi, throwing up to a dozen of explosives from the windows of the car towards shoppers. Then the SUVs crashed into shoppers, then collided with each other and exploded. The toll was a total of 43 deaths and more than 90 people in such suicide bombing and vehicular homicide.

May, 24, 2014, Belgium- most of the attacks perpetrated in Europe are driven by hatred to Western and no-Muslim culture. They don't have to be related to Islamic terrorist groups, therefore, they are unpredictable. The motive for the Belgium Jewish Museum Attack on Belgium are purely antisemitism, extremist Islamist beliefs. On May 24, a gunman opened fire at the Jewish Museum of Belgium in Brussels, Belgium, killing four (4) people. At the end of the month, few days later, a French national of Algerian origin, was arrested in connection with the shooting. He is known to have spent over a year in Syria and had links with radical Islamists. He had allegiance to the Islamic State of Iraq and Syria (ISIS).

July 28, 2014, China- attacks in southern Xinjiang, with 37 people dead and more than 13 people injured. Another time, when a gang armed with knives, well this time with axes too, attacked a police station and a government office. Suspects (18 of them) surrendered in Xinjiang Uyghur autonomous Region, to police after a major campaign encouraging the public to expose them. Police shot dead 59 of the attackers and arrested 215 others, confiscating banners proclaiming "holy war." August 2014, Syria- ISIL fighters massacred some 700 people of the Al-Shaitat tribe to try to take control of the Sunni area. The Islamic State fighters committed such massacre by shooting, beheading, and crucifying the 700 members of Shaitat tribe over a period of three days. It became the bloodiest single atrocity committed by the Islamic State in Syria.

September 23, 2014, Australia- an Afghan Australian stabbed two counter terrorism officers in Melbourne, Australia. He was an 18 year old, who had their passports cancelled due to fears that they would join Islamic State of Iraq and the Levant (ISIS). Haider, the attacker, reported to have attended the police station to discuss his cancelled passport, two police approached him in the car park, to discuss the situation, Haider produced a knife and slashed the Victorian officer across the arm. He, then, turned on the AFP officer and first stubbed him in the face and chest, then climbed on top of him and repeatedly stabbed him. The officers, then, shot the assaulter in the head.

With the intensity of Islamic Terrorist attacks, reports have been less important, and because of the similarity of the attacks.

October 5, 2014, Russia- Caucasus Emirate was the Islamic group responsible for this terrorist attack in the city of Grozny, Chechen Republic, Russia. A suicide bomb carried out by a 19-year-old man, who went to the town hall where an event was taking place, tried to pass the security check. Then, as the security officers were trying to search him, the bomb which the bomber, Opti Mudarov, was carrying, exploded. Five officers, along with the suicide bomber, were killed, while 12 others were injured. Total death 6, plus 12 injured.

October 20, 2014, Canada- Martin Couture-Rouleau was a francophone Canadian living with his parents at the time of the attack he perpetrated, he converted to Islam in the previous year, and was praying at a mosque regularly. On October 20, 2014, he conducted a terrorist Islamic attack on two Canadian Forces members, by hitting them and ramming them with a car in a shopping center parking lot. He has been seen sitting in his car and watching for over two hours before the attack. The government has called the attack as a terrorist act by ISIL-inspired terrorist. The motive was clearly a Jihadism act. October 22, 2014, Canada- another Canadian converted to Islam, Michael Zehaf-Bideau, was the perpetrator of another terrorist attack in the Canadian soil, that killed 2 (including him) and injured 3 people. He was a descendant of a Libyan-Canadian father. He visited Libya after he converted to Islam in 2004. The shooter attacked Corporal Natahn Cirillo, a Canadian soldier on ceremonial sentry duty; he killed him. He then entered the nearby parliament building, where members of the Parliament of Canada were attending caucuses. Trying to pass through security guards, he then escaped inside and start a shootout with parliament security personal. He got shot 31 times by six officers and died on the scene. Before the attacks, Zehaf-Bideau made a video related to the reasons for his attack to be connected "to Canada's foreign policy and in respect of his religious beliefs." While he was running from the security entrance in the hallway, pursued by officers, he passed by few offices and rooms where few senior parliaments' personalities were having meetings, one of them was the leader of the opposition, Thomas Mulcair, and other Members of parliament.

October 22, 2014, Israel- a Hamas terrorist ran his vehicle into a group of people waiting at a light rail station in Jerusalem, Israel. He killed 2 and injured 8 people. Hamas is an Islamic Resistance Movement that support and practice Jihadism through its militants. It was created in 1987, as a side creation and offshoot of the Egyptian Muslim Brotherhood. It is a Palestinian Islamic organization, with a strong military support from terrorists and Islamists. Co-founder Sheik Ahmed Yassin stated in 1987, that Hamas was founded to liberate Palestine from Israeli occupation and to establish an Islamic state where Israel is now. The Hamas Charter affirmed such statement in 1988. In 2006, Hamas used an underground cross-border tunnel to capture the Israeli soldier Gilad Shalit, holding him captive until 2011, when he was released in exchange for 1,027 Palestinian prisoners. Destroying tunnels was a primary objective of Israeli forces in 2014 Israel-Gaza conflict. In 2006, in the January's Palestinian parliamentary elections, Hamas won a majority in the Palestinian Parliament, defeating the Palestinian Liberation Organization PLO-affiliated Fatah party. Following the elections, the Quartet U.S., Russia, United Nations, and the European Union, made future foreign assistance to the Palestinian Authority upon the future government's commitment to non-violence, recognition of the state of Israel, and acceptance of previous agreements. Hamas rejected those changes, which led the Quartet suspending its foreign assistance program and Israel economic sanctions on the Hamas-led administration. Later on, Israel and Egypt imposed an economic blockade of the Gaza Strip, on the motive that Fatah forces were no longer providing security there.

November 5, 10, and 18, 2014- Israel- in the first attack, a Hamas operative deliberately drove a van at high speed into crown of people, killing 4 and injuring more than 13, the second attack was related to an Israeli soldier who was stabbed to death by a Lone wolf Jihadist; the third attack, on the 18th, a Jerusalem synagogue attack by Islamic Jihadists killed 5 and injured 7 civilians. They were two Palestinians men, attacked the praying congregates with axes, knives and a gun. Israeli authorities stated that "it is seemed the men had acted alone".

November 28, 2014, Nigeria- Boko Haram was responsible for another Terrorist attack in the region of Kano, Kano State, Nigeria, killing 120 people and injuring around 260 others. It was an attack at the central Mosque in Kano, the biggest city in the mainly Muslim Northern Nigeria during the Islamic insurgency in Nigeria. Two suicide bombers blew themselves up and gunmen opened fire on those who were trying to escape.

Boko Haram, is just another group of people wanting political power over people's beliefs of religious weakness. The big operators of Boko Haram just want a piece of land to govern.

December 1, 2014, United Emirates Arab- a woman stubs a 47-year-old American to death in a mall in Abu Dubai. She later plants a bomb outside the home of an Egyptian-American doctor, which was safely dismantled. December 4, 2014, Russia- a group of armed militants of the Jihadists organization Caucus Emirate attacked a traffic police checkpoint outside the city of Grozny, Chechnya, Russia. They killed three policemen, then occupied a press building and an abandoned school. 14 policemen and 11 militants and 1 civilian were killed. The Press House was also burned. In total 26 people dead including the 14 policemen, 11 Jihadist from Caucasus Emirate and the 1 civilian. December 9, 2014, Philippines- this blast killed at least 11 people and another 43 were injured. Most of the victims were students. The bomb occurred in a bus in front of the main entrance of Central Mindanao University, in Maramag, Bukidnon, Philippines. The Bangsamoro Islamic Freedom Fighters were suspected by Philippine authority to be behind the bombings. December 15-16, 2014, Australia- Sydney was the scene of an Islamic Jihadist attempt by a lone gunman. It was hostage crisis developed in the city of Sydney. A lone gunman, Man Haron Monis, held hostages ten customers and eight employees of a Lindt chocolate café at Martin Place in Sydney. The toll of this terrorist hostage attack were 3 dead and 4 injured.

December 16, 2014, Pakistan- at least 132 children died in this Islamic Jihadist attack, total 148 people altogether, and injuring 114 victims. Tehrik-i-Taliban Pakistan was responsible of this barbarian attack, when seven gunmen affiliated with this terrorist group conducted this terrorist attack on the Army Public School in the northwestern Pakistani city of Peshawar. They entered the school and opened fire on school staff and children, killing most of them, including 132 schoolchildren, ranging between the age of eight and eighteen. This was the deadliest terrorist attack ever to occur in Pakistan. December 16, 2014, Yemen- two car bombs exploded in Rada' district, Al Bayda Governate, Yemen, killing as many as 31 people, including 20 children. It was an attack intended to hit a home of Shiite rebel leader. It didn't make it to the target but did hit the school bus.

December 18, 2014, Nigeria- Boko Haram killed 32 men and kidnaped at least 185 women and children, storming the village of Gumsuri from different directions, the attackers yelled the words of "Allahu akbar". They burned down half of the village with petrol bombs. Then, they took women and children. December 18, 2014, Syria- Mass grave of 230 people, tribesmen killed by ISIS in Syria, found in Eastern Syria. December 20 and 21, 2014, France- the 20th December's first attack involved a man yelling "Allahu Akbra" stabbed a police officer with a knife. Later on, he was killed. Toll was of the one (1) perpetrator killed, plus 3 police officer injured. The second act was similar to the first one; a man yelling Allahu Akbar ran over 11 pedestrians with his vehicle. Total of injuries was 11 people wounded.

December 22, 2014, Nigeria- Boko Haram insurgents made another attack in the Nigerian soil country, bombing a bus station in the city of Gombe, killing at least 20 people. December, 2014, Iraq- ISIL militants execute 150 women because they don't want to marry their fighters, and some of them were already pregnant. Same month, the 24th, a suicide bomber killed 33 people and wounded 55 others in the Baghdad area. December 25, 2014, Somalia- another Terrorist Islamic attack in Mogadishu, Somalia, left 9 dead from the Jihadist group Al-Shabbab. December 28, 2014, Cameroon- one of the first attacks of Boko Haram in Cameroon left a death tool of 30 dead.

2014 was one of the deadliest Jihadist Islamic attacks the world have seen in years. It was also a preparation for the worst; 2015 has a worse and bigger number of terrorist attacks. For 2014, 34 attacks were registered as prominent media covered attacks, receiving significant coverage. Other attacks has also been the center of attention, but were not presented here. During 2014, death toll was more than 2,033 people, and lot more than 1,189 injured people.

2015

January 5, 2015, Afghanistan- Taliban claimed responsibility for the killing of one (1) person and wounding more than 16 others. It was a car packed with explosives, drove up to the headquarters of EUPOL Afghanistan,a European police-training organization, in Kabul and detonated. EUPOL is a European Union mission to support and train police in Afghanistan, and improve the rule of Law. January 6- 2015, Iraq- two suicide bombers attacked a mosque in the town of Al-Jubba while Iraqi soldiers were resting, killing ten (10) soldiers plus the two attackers. Clashes after the bombings left other 13 security personnel dead and 21 wounded. Total of casualties were 25 deaths with more than 21 injured. January 7-9, 2015, France- Islamic State and Al-Qaeda in the Arabian Peninsula were the perpetrators of these barbaric attacks, a series of five attacks occurred across the ile-de-France region, particularly in Paris. The attacks killed 17 people, in addition to the three perpetrators, Said and Cherif Kouachi, and Amedy Coulibaly, and wounding 22 others. It was an attack planned many years ahead, claimed the terrorists. Two gunmen attacked the headquarters of the satirical newspaper Charlie Hebdo, killing twelve and injuring others before escaping, then later on, caught by police. At the time of the attacks, it was the deadliest act of terrorism in France since 1961 Virty-Le-Francois train bombing by the Organization de l'armee secrete (OAS). The primary motive behind the shooting is said to be the Charlie Hebdo cartoons making fun of numerous Islamic leaders, and drawings of Mahomet (Islam Prophet). January 8, 2015, Nigeria- Boko Haram, the terrorist Islamic organization have killed at least 200 people in the Baga massacre. It was a series of mass killings carried out by jihadists affiliated with Boko Haram, in the Nigerian two of Baga and its surroundings. The attack began on January 3rd when Boko Haram overran a military base that was the headquarters of the Multinational Joint Task Force containing troops from Chad, Niger and Nigeria. Several western media reported, over 2000 people are thought to have been killed or unaccounted for. Baga and at least 16 other towns are thought to have been destroyed as over 35,000 people are reported to have been displaced, with many feared to have drowned while trying to cross Lake Chad and others trapped on islands in the lake. The attacks are said to have resulted in Boko Haram extending its control to over 70% of Borno State, while its leader, Abubakar Shekau, claimed responsibility for the massacre in a video statement, saying that they "were not much" and that the group's insurgency would not stop. January 9, 2015, France- the Porte de Vincennes siege occurred at a Hypercacher Kosher superette in Porte de Vincennce in the wake of the Charlie Hebdo shooting two days earlier. It was when the two Charlie Hebdo gunmen were cornered. Amedy Coulibaly had pledged allegiance to the Islamic State of Iraq and the Levant (ISIS), and was a close friend of the Kouachi brothers. Armed with a submachine gun, an assault rifle and tow Tokarev pistols, Amedy Coulibaly entered and attacked the people in the kosher food superette. He killed four Jewish hostages, and held fifteen other hostages during the siege. The police ended the siege by storming the store and killing Coulibaly. 5 people died and 9 injured. January 10, 2015, Lebanon- 9 people died and more than 30 people injured in the 2015 Jabal Mohsen suicide. Two suicide bombers blew themselves up in a crowded café in Jabal Mohsen, Tripoli, Lebanon. After the first explosion, the second suicide bomber approached the Abu Imran café and shouted "allahu akbar". Before he could blow himself up, 60-year-old father of seven, his name Abu Ali, rushed and tackled the bomber, and prevented many deaths. The Al-Qaeda affiliated terrorist group Nusra Front took responsibility for the attacks, which targeted members of the Alawite civilians, followers of a branch of Shia Islam. The interior minister of Lebanon said that the attack was carried out by the Islamic State of Iraq and the Levant (ISIS). The Nusra is a Sunni Islamist militia fighting against Syrian Government forces in the Syrian Civil War, with the aim of establishing an

Islamist state in the country. It is the Syrian branch of Al-Qaeda. It was designed first as, the most successful arm of the rebel forces, then, the U.S. designated al-Nusra as a foreign terrorist organization, followed by the U.N. and many other countries. As of 2015, al-Nusra cooperates with Islamist and Jihadist rebel groups, and some Free Syrian Army-aligned groups, against Syrian government forces. January 29, 2015, Egypt- North Sinai was the location of this terrorist attack, executed by the Islamic State of Iraq and the Levant (ISIS). Militants from the ISIL-affiliated Wilayat Sinai militant group launched a series of attacks on army and police bases in Arish using car bombs and mortars. The attacks that occurred in more than 6 places, resulted in 44 deaths, and hundreds injured. January 30, 2015, Pakistan- another suicide bomb targeting Shiites, resulted in the death of at least 55 people, and injuring more than 59, in a Shiite mosque attack in southern Pakistan.

February 13, 2015, Pakistan- an attack during a Friday Prayer in a suburb of Peshawar, in a Shiite mosque, killed more than 19 and injured more than 40 people. It was a heavily armed operation executed by militants, resulting in such atrocity. February 14-15, 2015, Denmark- Copenhagen attack occurred on Valentine's Day, killing two victims and the suspected perpetrator, while five officers were wounded. A gunman opened fire at a café and later at the Great Synagogue in Copenhagen, killing two civilians and injuring five others.

March 7, 2015, Nigeria- a series of five blasts carried out by suicide bombers on the same day in five different areas in the city of Maiduguri, Borno State, Nigeria. According to official sources, 58 people were killed and more than 143 others injured in the attacks. No terrorist group claimed responsibility for the blasts, but various sources blamed Boko Haram as the attacks were similar to the ones this Islamic Terrorist group perform.

March 15, 2015, Pakistan- suicide bombers kill at least 15 people in attacks on two churches in Lahore. A pair of suicide bombers attacked two churches outside the eastern Pakistani city on Sunday as worshippers prayed inside, killing innocent people in an assault against religious minorities in this increasingly fractured country. Afterward, an angry Christian mob blocked a major highway, ransacked a bus terminal and burned two people to death who they suspected of being involved in the attacks. Christian demonstrators blocked roads in other major Pakistani cities as well. The explosions occurred at the two churches while parishioners worshipped at Sunday morning services. Three days later, March 18, 2015, Tunisia- Islamic militants linked to the Islamic State of Iraq and Levant (ISIL or ISIS) were responsible for the Barbo National Museum attack. The terrorist act result in the death of 24 people and about 50 more people wounded. Three terrorist attacked the Barbo National Museum in Tunis, the Tunisian capital, and looked for hostages. ISIL claimed responsibility for the attack, and threatened to commit further attacks. The attack resulted on the death of 20 foreign tourists. The attack began at around noon. The tourists were attacked as they were getting off a bus to enter the Barbo Museum compound. At that time, security guards protecting the museum and the nearby Parliament building were absent on a coffee break!!! As many visitors ran toward the museum to avoid the shooting, the attackers, using Kalashnikov rifles and Hand grenades, pursued them and took them hostage inside. The siege lasted three hours, ending when security forces breached the building and killed two of the attackers. March 20- 2015, Yemen- the Islamic State of Iraq and the Levant (ISIL) claimed responsibility for the four Sana'a mosque suicide bombings, in the capital of Yemen, killing 142 and injuring more than 351, making the deadliest attack in Yemen's history. In a recording released by the group, they stated: "IS soldiers will not rest until they stop the Safawi (Iranian) operation in Yemen." Al-Qaeda in the Arabian Peninsula (QAP) denied responsibility, citing instructions from Ayman al-Zawahiri to not attack mosques or markets. It was the first attack carried out by ISIL in Yemen. The targeted mosques are linked to the Houthis, a group sect of Shia Islam. The Houthis deposed the Yemeni government earlier in 2015 after they took control of Sana'a the previous year. The Houthis is a very dangerous -unhuman- Islamist Terrorist group, operating from 1994 till present. Its logo reads "God (Allah) is Great, Death to America, Death to Israel, Curse on the Jews, Victory to Islam." The logo is a definition of pure hatred to humanity and its ideology should be banned from earth. It mostly operate in Yemen and Southern Saudi Arabia. The group was founded by Hussein al-Houthi, a Shia-leader, who started a rebellion in 2004 which led to a Houthi insurgency in Yemen against the President, Ali Abdullah Saleh. The Houthis participated in the 2011 Yemeni Revolution. In 2014-15 Houthis took over the government in Sana's, which led to the fall of the Saudi Arabian-backed government of Hadi. Houthis and their allies gained control of a significant part of Yemen's territory and are currently resisting the Saudi Arabian-led intervention in Yemen seeking to restore Hadi in power. Both the Houthis and Saudi Arabian-led coalition are being attacked by the Islamic State terrorist group. It is a real conclusion of how the Arab Spring revolution helped many Terrorist fanatic groups to use people and the moment of these revolts and protestations for their own benefits.

March 25, 2015, Libya- ISIL affiliates, the Shura Council of Benghazi Revolutionaries in Libya carried out suicide bombings in the city of Benghazi, killing 12 and injuring more than 25 people.

After the revolution that took Libyan President Muammar Gaddafi, Libya have been the scene of many conflicts that led to un-unified country. From 1969 to 2011, Gaddafi was a Libyan revolutionary and politician who govern Libya as its primary leader. He took power in a coup d'état in 1969. After 1011, Libya went through many changes, which are still shaping its destiny. Khalifa Haftar is a Libyan general and the principal commander of one side in the ongoing Libyan Civil War of 2014. He served in the Libyan army under Muammar Gaddafi, and took part in the coup he commanded the Libyan contingent against Israel in the Yorm Kippur War of 1973. He was held prisoner during the war against Chad. While in prison, he and his fellow officers formed a group hoping to overthrow Gaddafi. He was released around 1990 in a deal with United States government and spent about two decades in the United States, gaining U.S. citizenship.

How a general who has been responsible for the killing of Israelis during a war be awarded the U.S. citizenship? Politic, or conspiracy!!!

In 1993, Haftar, later on, was convinced in absentia of crimes against the Jamahiriya (the Libyan Republic), and sentenced to death. He held a senior position in the forces which overthrow Gaddafi in the 2011 Libyan Civil War. In 2014, he was commander of the Libyan Army when the General National Congress (GNC) refused to give up power in accordance with its term. He launched a campaign against the GNC and its Islamic fundamentalist allies. The campaign allowed elections to take place to replace GNC, but then developed into a civil war. The Shura Council of Benghazi Revolutionaries was formed in the wake of the Second Libyan Civil War. It is a military coalition in Benghazi composed of Islamist and Jihadist militias. The group was initially formed in June 2014, in response both to the anti-Islamist Operation Dignity being led by Khalifa Haftar, and also the defeat of Islamist candidates in the 2014 Council of Deputies election.

March 27, 2015, Somalia- on that day, the Islamic Jihadist group of Al-Shabbab and its insurgents attacked the Hotel Makka Al Mukarama in Mogadishu, the capital. It was an attack by Islamists Terrorists that drove a detonated car filled with explosives, then followed by other five armed militants who penetrated the grounds in another vehicle. A number of government officials and foreigners were staying at the hotel at the time. The attack resulted in the death of more than 20 people and wounding more than 28.

April 2, 2015, Kenya- another attack by Al-Shabbab, claimed the lives of more than 152 and injuring 79. The attack happened at Garissa University College. The gunmen took over 700 students' hostage, freeing Muslims and killing those who identified as Christians. Some students were rescued by soldiers, who described the presence of at least five masked, armed gunmen, as well as Christians being "shot on the spot". Two days after the attacks, Al-Shabbab issued a statement in English aimed at the Kenyan public. The attack had the purpose of scaring the Kenyan government of possible more attacks by denouncing what it described as "unspeakable atrocities against the Muslims of East Africa" by Kenyan security forces. April 8, 2015, Saudi Arabia- ISIL is blamed to be behind the shooting and killing of two policemen in the city of Riyadh. April 14, 2015, Somalia- another attack by Al-Shabbab, Al-Qaeda affiliate; this time on a government building in Mogadishu in the Ministry of Higher Education. 17 dead and 15 injured. April 17, 2015, Iraq- series of bombings in different areas in Bagdad, and a car bombing at the entrance of the US consulate in Erbil, resulted in the death of more than 43, and 64 wounded. ISIL claimed responsibility for these (routine) attacks on the Iraqi soil. April 18, 2015, Afghanistan- a suicide bomb detonated in front of a bank in Jalalabad. ISIL claimed responsibility for the death of 33 people and wounding more than 100. April 19, 2015, France- a gunman trying to attack a church was stopped, but killed a (1) Frenchwoman before he got arrested. April 20, 2015, Somalia- Al-Shabbab Islamic Jihadist group bombed a minivan of United Nation's workers in the Puntland region of Somalia, killing 9 and wounding 4 people. Al-Shabaab is a militant Islamic group created in 2006. Al-Shabaab is an Arabic word which means the Youth or the Youngsters. It is a Jihadist Islamic group based in East Africa. As of 2015, the group has retreated from the major cities, controlling a few rural areas.

April 27, 2015, Bosnia and Herzegovina- an Islamic extremist fueled with anger attacked a police station. He killed one officer and wounded two others before he was shot dead by other police officers. According to the investigation, the 24 years' old terrorist was asked not to park in front of the station, he then opened fire with his rifle, shouting Allahu Akbar (God is Great). He was a member of one of the most fanatic Islamic groups, the Wahhabi movement. Today Wahhabism's teachings are state-sponsored and are the official form of Sunni Islam in 21st century's Saudi Arabia. Estimates of the numbers of adherents to Wahhabism vary, with some giving a figure fewer than 5 million Wahhabis in the Persian Gulf region (compared to 28.5 million Sunnis and 89 million Shia). With the help of funding from petroleum exports, the movement underwent major growth beginning in the 1970s and now has worldwide influence. It has been seen as the source of global terrorism, inspiring the ideology of the Islamic State of Iraq and Syria (ISIS), and for causing disunity in the Muslim communities, by labeling some who disagree with them with monotheism or apostates.

May 3, 2015, Iraq- ISIS (Islamic State of Iraq and Syria) claimed responsibility for the two car bombs that were detonated this day, just ten minutes from each other, taking the lives of 19 people. Same day, in a retaliation for depictions of Muhammad (Islam religion's prophet), two gunmen attacked the Curtis Culwell Center during a cartoon exhibit, in Garland, Texas. The attack was carried out by militants affiliated to ISIS. The attackers shot officers with gunfire at the entrance of the exhibit featuring cartoon images of "prophet" Muhammad. After the attackers pulled up and opened fire, both were shot and killed by a police officer. On Twitter website, minutes before the attack, one of the gunmen posted "May Allah accept us as mujahedeen". Two mistakes; first, Allah doesn't exist; second, the concept of "mujahedeen" is and was a political creation to beneficiate the need for some entities, governments, particulars, political forces, kings or Presidents, to establish a more controllable censure of the people. It is a political concept to gather people under one belief, and distract them from other issues. Issues that can withdraw attention toward the ones that govern the society. This concept "mujahedeen" must be abolished, and every group or organization calling themselves by the name of God, Allah or Jihad must be censured and eliminated. Such organizations or groups should be banned from operating under such concept, and should be given the opportunity to turn its concept to a more economic and productive domain.

On February 5, 2016, according to CNN, Company Twitter says it has suspended 125,000 accounts for threatening or promoting terrorist acts.

On May 3rd attack, it was the first time the militant group of Islamic State of Iraq and Syria (ISIL or ISIS) took credit for, and claimed responsibility for an attack in the United States.

Same day, May 3, 2015, Afghanistan- Taliban militants overran checkpoints in Warduj, district of Badakhshan Province in eastern Afghanistan. 17 people died, all of them policemen. Next day, May 4, 2015, Afghanistan- a government bus was attacked by a suicide bomber in Kabul, killing 1 person and wounding 15 others. May 10, 2015, Iraq- same scenario happened a week ago, two car bombs were detonated ten minutes apart in Baghdad, and surrounding. ISIS claimed responsibility for the attacks, killing 14 and injuring more than 30. May 10, 2015, Afghanistan- a bus carrying Afghan government employees was attacked in Kabul by a suicide bomber, killing 3 people and wounding more than 10, in an attack in which Taliban claimed responsibility. May 13, 2015, Pakistan- a bus carrying Shia Muslims was attacked by six armed gunmen who rode up in motorcycles. The toll of dead people reached 45, with more than 13 injured. Some Islamist groups claimed responsibility for this attack on religious minorities. The vehicle was carrying men, women and children from the Ismaili Muslim community, a Shiite sect. unlike some other Shiite groups, Ismailis hadn't been heavily targeted by militants in Pakistan previously. It proves that things are different now, and nobody is safe or exhorted from either sides. Shiite and Sunni Muslims have been fighting each other's in a more violent ways than before. Sunni and Shia Islam are the two major denominations of Islam. Sunnis are a majority in most Muslim communities: in Southeast Asia, China, South Asia, Africa and most of the Arab world. Shia make up the majority of the citizen population in Iraq, Iran, Azerbaijan, and Bahrain, as well as being a politically significant minority in Lebanon. Sunnis are a majority among Muslims in the United States. However, the majority of Arab Muslims in the United States are Shia, while the majority of Arab Americans are Christians, the conflation of Arab and Muslim being quite common.

Shias make up the majority of the Muslim population in Iran (around 95%, 74 million Shiite), Iraq (75%, with close to 28 million population Shiite), and Bahrain (around 70%) and Azerbaijan (around 90%). Bahrain and Azerbaijan are both relatively small countries compared to Iraq or Iran, Bahrain's population is just close 1.4 million, while Azerbaijan's population was estimated at 9.6 million on 2015. With close to 79 million the population of Iran, it has the highest number of Shiites in the world. The history of Iran has been shaped dramatically during the last and present century. In 1941, Reza Shah was forced to abdicate in favor of his son, Mohammad Reza Pahlavi, and established the Persian Corridor, a massive supply route that would last until the end of the ongoing war. In 1951, Mohammad Mosaddegh was elected as the prime minister, he was known by his democracy advocacy. He became enormously popular in Ira, after he nationalized Iran's petroleum industry and oil reserves. He was deposed in the 1953 coup d'état, an Anglo-American covert operation that marked the first time the US had overthrown a foreign government during the Cold War.

After the coup, Iran has entered a phase of decade's long controversial foreign governments. While the Shah increasingly modernized Iran, arbitrary arrests and torture by his secret police were used to crush all forms of political opposition. Ayatollah Ruhollah Khomeini became an active critic, and publicly denounced the government for its ties with US. Khomeini was arrested for 18 months, then released, then sent into exile. He went first to Turkey, then Iraq, and finally to France. Due to the 1973 spike in oil price, the economy of Iran was flooded with foreign currency, which caused inflation. By 1974, the economy was in a bad shape, despite many large projects to modernize the country. By 1975 and 1976, am economic recession led to increased unemployment, especially among young people. By the late 1970s, many of the Iranians opposed the Sha's regime and began to organize and join the protests against him. Khomeini then returned to Iran after 14 years exile, on February 1, 1979. Major protestations began in January 1978 against the Shah. After a year of strikes and demonstrations, Mohammad Reza Pahlavi fled the country and Khomeini returned, forming a new government. Iran, then, became an Islamic republic, after holding a referendum. The transformation from a civilized country to an Islamic "terrorist" had begun. The revolution, which started in 1980, imposed an initial closure of universities for three years, in order to perform an inspection and cleanup in the cultural policies of the education and training system. On September, Iran invaded the Iranian Khuzestan, and the Iran-Iraq War began. At the end of 1979, a group of students seized the US Embassy and took hostage of 52 personnel and citizens. Among the demands was to send back Mohammad Reza Pahlavi to Iran for a trial. The US refused to return him back to Iran. Jimmy Carter (US President) administration tried to negotiate for the release of the hostages and failed, forcing Carter out of office and brought Ronald Reagan to power. The last hostages were finally set free on Carter's final day in office. The 1979 Revolution was later known as the Islamic Revolution. Iran, nowadays, have a very active role in the world's political strategies. It is a country showing the world that the base of its foreign relations is orientated on two strategic principles: eliminating outside influences in the region and pursuing extensive diplomatic contacts with developing and non-aligned countries. However, the reality is a way different, and Iran, like most other Middle East countries and North African countries, specially Kingdoms like Morocco, where King Mohammed VI do whatever he please to, help the spread of Islamic fanatics, Jihadism and hatred to other religions for the sole purpose of staying in power. Their Presidents and kings have only one worry, and it is how to stay in power as long as an eternity. They are using religion to keep the population following their leadership, regardless of the price people have to pay. Governments in all those countries chose to minimize any developments for their citizens and focus only on the elites, leaving populations live with very limited resources. For that reason, they are called the Third World Countries. The sacrifice can be at home, means inside their own countries, examples from bad or unfavorable economy, poor life condition, lack of jobs, weak healthcare for their people, to a nonexistence conditions of development. Or, even a more tragic sacrifice can be presented abroad their own countries, and that is when they go and expatriate their hatred in other foreign countries, examples like killing innocent people under the name of "Allah" or religion. In both cases, governments, Presidents and Kings (Mohammed VI for instance) are responsible for both results, domestic or abroad.

May 14, May 17, May 19, May 25, 2015, Afghanistan- in the first attack, a hotel that was hosting a cultural event was attacked by Taliban fighters in Kabul killing 14 people including an American, an Italian and four Indians. In the second attack, Taliban, again, execute a suicide attack near the entrance of Hamid Karzai International Airport targeting a European police training vehicle, killing 3 and wounding 18 people. In the thirst attack, May 19th, a suicide car bombing detonated in the parking lot of a Justice

Ministry building in the diplomatic section of Kabul, leaving 4 people dead and wounding more than 42. The fourth attack of this month in Afghanistan was the work (again) of the Taliban militants which killed 19 policemen and 6 soldiers during a siege at a police compound in Nawzad District of Afghanistan. In the duration of one month, Taliban have succeeded on the planning and execution of four "unhuman" attacks against people, under the name of Islam. This should be unacceptable and stopped, regardless of the motives or needs. Afghanistan's government should get punished for allowing such atrocities, and Islam as a religion can't justify such killings; no excuse.

May 21, 2015, Libya- a suicide bomber detonated his explosives at a military checkpoint outside Misrata, North east Libya, killing himself and two guards. May 22, 2015, Saudi Arabia- ISIS claimed responsibility for this attack, targeting Shia mosque during prayer. It happened when a suicide bomber attacked the Shia mosque in the al-Qadeeh village, killing 21 worshippers and injuring more than 90 others. More than 150 people were praying when the huge explosion ripped through the Imam Ali mosque in a packed Shi'ite mosque in eastern Saudi Arabia. May 26, 2015, Kenya- another attack by Al-Shabaab militants in Kenya. They attacked two police patrols which turned into a gun battle north Garissa, Kenya. 5 police officers were injured while they were fighting the attackers which got killed in the fight. May 28, 2015, Iraq- two car bombs were set off minutes apart targeting the Cristal Grand Ishtar and the Babylon, killing 10 and injuring 30 people. May 29, 2015, Saudi Arabia- another attack at a mosque, a Shia mosque in Dammam, the capital of Eastern Province, Saudi Arabia. ISIS claimed responsibility for this suicide bomber. The suicide bomber disguised as a woman blew himself up by detonating the bomb in the parking lot, resulting in the death of 4 people, and an undisclosed number of non-fatal injuries.

June 1, 2015, Iraq- three suicide attacks in Iraq's Anbar kill 41 from security forces. In such attacks, ISIS targeted a police base in Iraq's western Anbar province with explosives-laden Humvees. The IS group and other Sunni extremists view Shiites as apostates deserving of death.

So, basically both parties; Sunnis and Shiites point fingers at each other's blaming each other's for being apostates. Why don't they just get over it and accept that both aren't apostates!!! They are just different. If both are proud of their religion –Islam-, well, they should actually like each other's. They go even as far as killing other people for not believing in God. As a result of such conflict, they are just ignorant and hopeless. Religion is just an excuse for military power, and political influence. Sunnis view Shiites as apostates, and Shiites view Sunnis as apostates is just endless nonsense. The main purpose is acquiring lands and political power, while the main weapon is religion. On May, there was more than 1,031 people killed and another 1,648 wounded in violence across Iraq. The U.N. figures in Iraq, showed that 665 civilians and 366 members of the Iraqi security forces were killed in May.

June 5, 2015, Turkey- ISIS was responsible for the bombing that occurred on that Sunday. It took place two days before the June 2015 general election and killed 4 supporters, injuring more than 100 people. The bombing was targeting a rally organized by the Peoples' Democratic Party (HDP) supporters. Suspicions as for the perpetrators still lie on ISIL.

ISIL is a Terrorist Islamic group, established in 1999, under the name of Jama'at al-Tawhid wal- Jihad, still operating under ISIL or ISIS. It joined al-Qaeda in October 2004, then declared the creation of an Islamic State in Iraq in 2006. In 2013, the claimed territory in the Levant. The Levant composed of countries and regions in the Middle East, precisely a large area in the eastern Mediterranean, they are: Cyprus, Israel, Jordan, Lebanon, Palestine,

Syria and Turkey (Hatay Province). In February 2014, ISIL separated itself from al-Qaeda, then on June same year, they declared the creation of caliphate. November 2014, they claimed territories in: Libya, Egypt, Algeria, Saudi Arabia and Yemen. Then, January 2015, they claimed territory in Afghanistan, Pakistan and parts of Libya. March 2015, they claimed territory in Nigeria and then June 2015, they claimed North Caucasus as part of their territory. This Organization is a Salafi jihadist militant group that follows an Islamic fundamentalist, Wahhabi doctrine of Sunni Islam. The group is also known as Daesh, which is an acronym derived from its Arabic name ad-Dawlah al-Islamiyah fi l-Iraq wa-sh-Sham. It proclaimed itself as a worldwide caliphate, claiming religious, political and military authority over all Muslims worldwide. The group has control over vast landlocked territory in Iraq and Syria, with a population estimate ranging between 3 million and 8 million people and where it enforces its interpretation of Sharia law (the most barbaric law of Islam). The numbers of fighters the group commands in Iraq and Syria was estimated between 31,000 and 40,000 fighters, majority Syrian and Iraq nationals.

June 13, 2015, Iraq- four suicide car bombs went off in an Iraqi station near Tikrit, killing 11 and wounding more than 27 people.

June 26, 2015, France- another religious motivated hatred attack by a lone French Muslim of North African descent, motivated by ISIS, decapitated his employer Herve Cornara and drove his van into gas cylinders at a gas factory in Saint-Quentin-Fallavier near Lyon, France. 1 dead and 2 injured in the attacks. Same day, Turkey- 27 people were killed in an explosion at a Shia mosque, Imam Sadiq mosque, in Kuwait City. The attack was claimed by ISIS. Same day, Tunisia- 2015 Sousse attack was against two tourist hotels, resulted in the death of more than 38 people. An armed gunman attacked a hotel, disguised as a tourist, socialized with others, and then took out a Kalashnikov assault rifle concealed in a beach umbrella and fired at the tourists on the beach. He entered the hotel, shooting at people he came across. He was killed by security forces during an exchange of fires. Thirty of the dead casualties were British. Same say, Somalia- an attack occurred by Al-Shabaab terrorist group against the African Union Mission to Somalia, resulted in a 70 plus deaths and losses with a 27 injured victims casualties. June 26-30, 2015, Nigeria- Boko Haram kills at least 200 people as they gun down and bomb villages, mosques and other public spaces. That day of June 26, 2015, has seen 5 attacks in 5 different countries in one day; France, Kuwait, Tunisia, Somalia and Nigeria. June 29, 2015, Israel- Hamas came back to the scene after this attack, when a Hamas gunmen opened fire on a civilian vehicle. Four occupants in the car were wounded and rushed to hospital, where one (1) died.

July 5, July 7, 2015, Nigeria- first attack consisted of a two bombs that exploded at an elite restaurant and mosque, killing at least 15 people in the city of Jos, Plateau State, in the Middle Belt of Nigeria. Second bomb occurred in a government office in Zaria, Kaduna State, Nigeria, killing 20 people. July 13, 2015, Cameroon- Boko Haram suspected in two suicide attacks that killed at least 12 civilians and a Chadian soldier in the northern Cameroon town of Fotokol. Boko Haram, which launched an insurgency six years ago to create an emirate in northern Nigeria, has also stepped up attacks in neighboring Chad, Cameroon and Niger in recent months. It shows how an idea –terrorism Jihad- can be shaped to affect other surrounding countries. July 17, 2015, Nigeria- at least 64 people, including two suicide bombings, in multiple blasts in the northeastern Nigerian towns of Gombe and Damaturu. Two female suicide bombers killed 12 people at two prayer grounds in Damaturu on Friday morning as people were preparing to celebrate the end of Ramadan, the Muslim holy month of fasting. Few hours earlier, two bombs killed 50 people buying goods for the holiday at the market in Gombe. Another 75 wounded people were among the casualties. The attacks were blamed on Nigeria's homegrown Boko Haram armed terrorist group, which has launched a series of attacks that have killed hundreds during the Muslim holy month of Ramadan, which ended Friday. The upsurge in attacks followed a directive from the Islamic State in Iraq and the Levant (ISIS) to create more mayhem during the month of Ramadan. Boko Haram had sworn allegiance to ISIL, intensifying its attacks in the few months before and after these attacks. July 20, 2015, Turkey-suicide bombing killed 33 people and injured 104 in the Kurdish majority city of Suruc, Turkey. ISIL claimed responsibility. July 22, 2015, Nigeria- more bombings and explosions in Nigeria, in Gombe, killed 40 people. Two bus stations where the explosions occurred mark the second deadly bombing to hit the northeastern city of Gombe in less than a week. July 26, 2015, Cameroon- at least 14 people have been killed after a female suicide bomber detonated an explosive at a popular night spot in the town of Maroua in northern Cameroon. A week before the attack, in a separate blast in the same town, two young girls detonated explosives they were wearing and killed at least 20 people. While there was no immediate claim of responsibility, fighters from Boko Haram have been blamed for scores of attacks in the region this year. They are the only Terrorist group capable of such atrocity in the region, fueled by hatred and support form ISIL. August 11, 2015, Nigeria-more than 50 people were killed and more than 50 injured as explosions erupted at a crowded market in the town of Sabon Gari, in Borno state, which is the heartland of the Boko Haram armed group. Boko Haram has killed thousands of people during a seven-year armed campaign to establish an Islamic state in northeastern Nigeria. August 13, 2015, Iraq- a truck bombed in a Baghdad market killed more than 76 people and wounded more than 212 others. ISIL claimed responsibility for the attack, stating that "God has enabled the soldiers of the Islamic State to detonate a parked, booby-trapped truck amid a gathering of apostates in one of their most important Shiite majority strongholds, in Sadr City". The attack targeted members of Iraq's Popular Mobilization Forces, largely comprising Shi'ite militias allied with the Iraqi government. The victims were innocent civilians. ISIL targeted the food market because of its predominantly Shi'ite neighborhood. August 21, 2015, France- another Islamic terrorist attack in a train occurred in France. The attack happened in a train on its way from Amsterdam to Paris. The perpetrator opened fire in a train carriage before being subdued by passengers, one of whom he stabbed. 4 people were injured. Ayoub EL Khazzani, a 25 year old man from Morocco, was identified as the suspected assailant by French and Spanish authorities. He lived in Spain form 2007 to 2014. During his stay in Spain, he attracted the attention of authorities after making speeches defending jihad, attending a known radical mosque, and being involved in drug trafficking. He then moved to France, at which time the Spanish authorities informed the French of their suspicions. He had reportedly spent time between May and July 2015 in Syria before moving to France. Prosecutors discovered files on his phone of a YouTube audio in which an individual exhorted his followers to raise arms and fight in the name of the prophet. He was listening to them immediately prior to the attack. He claimed he was a homeless looking for food and that he was hungry at the time of the attack. He said, his intentions were just to rub the passengers –which was a lie-, he was brain-washed with all the propaganda about how Islam is the true only religion (another big lie). He was a terrorist, a killer and radicalized Muslim.

August 28-30, 2015, Nigeria- during two days, Boko Haram members massacre 79 people in three different Nigerian villages. Gunmen on horseback shot dead 68 people in the attack on Baanu village in Borno state late on Friday while another 11 people were shot dead in two other villages on Saturday and Sunday. September 10, 2015, Nigeria- explosion at a refugee camp for people fleeing Boko Haram killed more than 2 people. Boko Haram's atrocities didn't stop at villages or cities, they go as far as killing innocent people escaping and living even in refugee camps!!!

September 17, 2015, Iraq- two bombing occurred in Baghdad, killing at least 10 people. The bombing went off in mainly Shia neighborhood in central Baghdad. They were carried out by bombers on foot, wearing explosives-laden vests. One struck in Baghdad's al-Sharji area, and the second struck at al-Wathda Square. The Islamic State of Iraq and the Levant (ISIL) terrorist group claimed responsibility for the bomb attacks. The targets were mainly Shia militia fighters and police. Since the emergence of ISIL, Baghdad has seen nearly a daily attack, with roadside bombs, suicide blasts and assassinations targeting Shia civilians, Iraqi forces and government officials, with significant casualties among the civilian population. The violence has killed hundreds and displayed tens of thousands of Iraqis.

September 17, 2015, Germany- an Islamist of Iraqi descent attacked and injured a police officer with a knife in Berlin. Cops, then, shot him dead the after he stabbed a policewoman in the street. The Terrorist Islamic believed to be a member of a terrorist organization. September 21, 2015, Nigeria- at least 54 people were killed by multiple explosions in Nigeria. The blasts occurred in the city of Maiduguri in Borno state, an area often targeted by Boko Haram fighters. The bombers detonated Improvised Explosives Devices (IEDs) at a mosque in Ajilari and some insurgents also threw IEDs at a viewing center. The blasts hit the country a day after a new audio message purportedly from Boko Haram leader Abubakar Shekau accused the army of lying about successes against the group. Maiduguri is the capital of Borno state, the birthplace of the brutal armed group of Boko Haram that plagued the oil-rich country with violence in recent years. The audio recording, said to be of Boko Haram's leader, criticized Nigeria's military for saying it had recaptured villages that had fallen to the group. More than 1,000 people have been killed by the Islamic group's violence since

President Buhari was inaugurated as president on May 2015, vowing to crush Boko Haram. Boko Haram's main purpose is to gain power, and own a piece of land, that can give its leader political and economic power (Nigeria has oil). Religion, Islam, is only a way for them to gain support from normal civilians, and to be legible to fight in the name of Allah (another mislead). Their excuse is a big lie to gain power, regardless of the price it costs (people's lives). September 24, 2015, Yemen- a bomb attack on a Shia mosque in Sana'a killed 25, and wounding more than 20 people. ISIL claimed responsibility for the attack. The bombs targeted Shia worshippers at a mosque in Yemen's capital during prayers for the Muslim holiday of Eid al-Adha. The Islamic State of Iraq and the Levant claimed responsibility and said the attacks were to strike the "Houthi infidels", in reference to the Shia rebels who have been in control of the capital for the past year. The blast happened in the Balili mosque where Houti rebels who control Sana'a go to pray. September 29, 2015, Bangladesh- three men on a motorbike shot and killed an Italian aid worker, in an attack that have been claimed by ISIL.

October 1, 2015, Nigeria- more attacks by suicide bombings killed 14 people and injured more than 39 people, perpetrated by Boko Haram in North-East Nigeria. October 1, 2015, Israel- gunmen opened fire on a car near Nablus on the northern West Bank, killing a man and woman. Witnessing the attack, 4 kids were also inside the car, but didn't get hurt in the attack. Hamas, inhumanly and in-understandably, praised the attackers. October 2, 2015, Australia- a 15-year old Terrorist Muslim lone gunman, shot to death a civilian Police officer employee, then engaged with the Police Force Special Constables in a shootout before being killed. October 3, 2015, Bangladesh- four days earlier an Italian aid worker was shot and killed by an ISIS member. With a similar faith, this time to a Japanese aid worker, who was shot and killed in a similar way by ISIS. October 3, 2015, Iraq- another attack claimed by ISIS for two suicide bombings in Shiite majority neighborhoods killed at least 18 people and injured more than 61. October 5, 2015, Afghanistan- Taliban came back to the Jihadism Islamic scene by these two suicide bombings in Kabul, targeting an Afghan intelligence center. Casualties were of 3 people injured. October 7, 2015, Somalia- Militants of Al-Shabaab ambushed and killed a relative of Somalia's president, his nephew. The toll was of 2 deaths. October 10, 2015, Turkey- ISIS was blamed for these 2015 Ankara bombings, where 102 people died and more than 400 others wounded. The incidents happened in front of the Ankara Central railway station, where two bombs were detonated. It was the deadliest of its kind in Turkey's modern history. October 10, 2015, Chad- various suicide bombings and mass murders perpetrated by ISIS and Boko Haram, resulted in the death of 38 people and non-fatal injuries of 51 others. The attacks occurred in a village in Chad in market area and refugee camp, in Baga Sola, Lac Region, Chad. October 11, 2015, Afghanistan- another bomb attack by Taliban in the same month in Kabul. This time, Taliban targeting a British military convoy, injured 7 Afghan civilians. October 22, 23, 2015- Nigeria- Boko Haram was the main suspect for a two days attacks in various places throughout Nigeria. The first attack killed 20 people in the northeast state of Borno. The second, targeting two separate mosques with suicide bombers, killing 42 and injuring about 200 people. The insurgency in the region has claimed at least 17,000 lives since 2009. October 28, 2015, Niger- Boko Haram militants attack a village in Niger, running down 13 people and allegedly burning down houses and cars during the rampage. They just ambush villages with no goal, but killing people. It does have one purpose, create chaos and insecurity within the society. So far, Boko Haram displaced 2.1 million people in the remote northeast of Nigeria. The biggest problem Niger have is controlling the border with Nigeria. Boko Haram could cross the borders anytime and kill people over the other side of the border. October 31, 2015, Egypt- Russia- ISIS claimed responsibility for the Metrojet Flight 9268 crash, that killed 224 people; 219 Russians, 4 Ukrainians, and one Belarussian. The flight was following its departure from Sharm el-Sheikh International Airport, Egypt, en route to Pulkovo Airport, Saint Petersburg, Russia. It was the deadliest crash in the history in both, the Russian aviation and within Egyptian territory. Egyptian authorities reported that the aircraft split in two and most bodies were found strapped to their seats. The Russians said they have found explosive residue as evidence, and it was a terrorist attack caused by improvised bomb containing the equivalent of up to 2.2 lb (1kg) of TNT that detonated during the flight.

November 12, 2015, Lebanon- two unidentified members of the Islamic State of Iraq and the Levant militants have been suspected for the two suicide explosive bombings that been detonated in Bourg el-Barajneh, a southern suburb of Beirut, that is inhabited mostly by Shia Muslims. ISIL claimed responsibility for the attacks that killed at least 42 people. November 13, 2015, France-this day incident was the most fatal event on French soil since World War II. It was a series of terrorist attacks in Paris that killed 137 people and wounded more than 368, all in different locations. The locations were all spread out around the city with a timeline that range from minutes to hours. The timeline of the attacks was as follow; November 13th- around 9:20pm, first suicide bombing near the Stade de Paris (an international soccer game was held at the same time). Around 9:21pm, shooting at the rue Bichat. Then 9:30pm, second suicide bombing near the Stade de France. 9:32pm, another shooting at the rue de la Fontaine-auRoi. 9:36pm, shooting at the rue de Charonne. 9:40pm a suicide bombing on boulevard Voltaire. 9:40pm, three men enter the Bataclan theatre and begin shooting. 9:53pm, third suicide bombing near the Stade de France. 10:00pm hostages are taken at the Bataclan. November 14th- 00:20am, security forces enter the Bataclan. 00:58am, French police end the siege on the Bataclan. Three terrorists' teams launched six distinct attacks: three suicide bombings in one attack, a fourth suicide bombing in another attack, and shootings at four locations in four separate attacks. The ISIL claimed responsibility for the attacks, saying that it was in retaliation for the French airstrikes on ISIL targets in Syria and Iraq. It was an act of war by ISIL planned in Syria, organized in Belgium and perpetrated with French complicity.

November 13, 2015, Iraq- a suicide bombing kills at least 21 at a Shia funeral. November 17, 2015, Philippines- a Malaysian national is beheaded by Abu Sayyaf's terrorist Islamic group in the southern Philippines. November 17, 2015, Nigeria- a suicide attack at a market in Yola, Nigeria, killed more than 30 people and injured more than 80, in an attack that been reported to be the work of Boko Haram. November 18, 2015, three Islamists in Marseille stabbed a Jewish history teacher in the arm and leg, "due to their beliefs". November 18, 2015, Bosnia and Herzegovina- a lone wolf Islamist gunman killed two (2) soldiers and injured civilians in Sarajevo. 3 people died and 5 injured in the attack. November 18, 2015, Nigeria- two explosions destroyed a phone market in Kano killing at least 15 people and injuring more than 100, in what authorities believe it's a work of Boko Haram. November 20, 2015, Niger- terrorist Islamist militants carrying guns, AK-47 assault rifles and hand grenades took more than 170 hostages and killed 20 of them in the Radisson hotel in Bamako, the capital city of Mali. Al-Mourabitoun claimed that it carried out the attack. Al Qaeda in the Islamic Maghreb was also of an asset with helping with the attacks. Al-Qaeda member confirmed that the two groups cooperated in the attack. Al-Mourabitoun militant group is an Islamic Terrorist group, operated from 2013 till present, with area of operations in countries as Algeria, Burkina Faso, Libya, Mali and Niger. It is an African militant jihadist organization formed by a merger between al-Tilemsi's Movement for Oneness and Jihad in West Africa and Mokhtar Belmokhtar's Masked Men Brigade. It is a branch of Al-Qaeda in the Islamic Maghred (AQIM) organization. In this attack, two gunmen arrived at the hotel, driving a vehicle with diplomatic license plates. Malian authorities said at least 10 gunmen had stormed the hotel shouting "Allahu Akbar" before firing on guards and taking hostages. Following the Libyan Civil War, many ethnic Tuareg who had fought for the Gaddafi government and the rebels took their weapons, then left for the Northern Mali, wants to be an independent state. The secular movement was soon overrun by Islamist-oriented groups such the Movement for Oneness and Jihad in West Africa (MOJWA) and Ansar Dine. The French launched a military operation that outsed the rebels, however, tensions and irregular incidents continued to occur. The Macina Liberation Front is a new Jihadist group, active from January 2015 till present, and is a Salafist Malian group aiming to restore the 19th Century Macina Empire. Through history, the Fulas of the region of Massina Empire, or Caliphate of Hamdullahi, had for centuries been the vassals of larger states, including the Mali Empire (13th-14th centuries), the Songhai Empire (15th century), the Moroccan pashas of Tamboctou (16th century), and the Bambara Empire at Segou (17th century). By early 1800s, early struggle created the Massina leadership and in 1818 Seku Amadu led a jihad against the Bambara Empire in 1818. The empire expanded and established a new capital at Hamdullahi in 1820. At the height of the Empire's power, it was by ordered "by Seku Amadu", the construction of six hundred Madrasas to further the spread of Islam. Alcohol, tobacco, music and dancing were banned in accordance with Islamic Law. Hundreds years later, 2015 seen the re-creation of the Macina Liberation Front, led by radical Muslim cleric Amadou Kouffa, a strong proponent of strict Islamic law in Mali. A Human Rights Watch report said the Macina Liberation Front militants had carried out serious abuses in parts of central Mali since January and killed at least five people they accused of being aligned to the Malian government.

November 20, 2015, Iraq- a suicide bomber detonates inside a Shiite mosque killing 10 people, while another bombings in other areas killed 5 others. November 21, 2015, Cameroon- Boko Haram responsible for the bombing and deaths of 10 people in northern Cameroon. November 22, 2015, Nigeria- a female suicide bomber detonated herself killing 8 people among children and other women. November 24, 2015, Tunisia- a bus transporting members of the Presidential Guard, in Tunis, exploded, killing 12, and injuring more than 16. ISIL (Islamic State of Iraq and the Levant) claimed responsibility for the attack. The bus was carrying members of the Tunisian Presidential Security guard. The explosion happened when the vehicle was parked near a main artery in the Tunisian capital where guard members are typically picked up and dropped off. November 24, 2015, Egypt- 7 dead and more than 10 injured in a terrorist attack on a hotel in the coastal city of Al-Arish, Egypt. It occurred the day after the second round of parliamentary elections closed, militants attack a hotel housing election judges in the provincial capital of al-Arish in Egypt's North Sinai. The perpetrators were ISIL and Wilayat Sinai (formerly known as Ansar Bait al-Maqdis). The latter is a branch of the Salafi jihadist group Islamic of Iraq and the Levant (ISIL). It is an active Islamic terrorist group in Egypt's Sinai Peninsula. The group was formed November 2014 following Sinai-based Ansar Bait al-Maqdis pledge of allegiance to ISIL. A group of militants approached the heavily guarded hotel with a car bomb, but Egyptian security forces opened fire at the vehicle, blowing it up before it could reach the building. One of the attackers managed to get inside the hotel, where a number of people were injured and killed as a result of gunfire and a subsequent suicide bombing. The Islamic State's Wilayat Sinai offshoot claimed responsibility in a statement released later the same day. November 25, 2015, Niger- Boko haram invades a village and shoots indiscriminately residents, attacked their homes and fire rockets at them, killing 18 people, including a local religious leader, in an attack on a village in Niger's southern border area of Diffa on the Nigerian border. The Islamist militants rarely claim attacks but they are based in the north of Nigeria and often launch cross border attacks in Niger, Chad and Cameroon. November 27, 2015, Nigeria-

Boko Haram attacks more and more Shia civilians. At least 21 people were killed in a suicide bomb attack on a Shia Muslim procession in the northern Nigerian state of Kano. November 28, 2015, Egypt- Islamist gunmen killed four security personnel in an attack at a police checkpoint in Saqqara, south of Cairo, near some of Egypt's historic pyramid sites, killing 4 people. The two attackers were riding a motor bike when they opened fire using machine guns at a police checkpoint in Saqqara, 22 miles south of Cairo. A militant group affiliated to Islamic State in Egypt claimed responsibility for the attack in a statement later. November 28, 2015, Mali- militants fired rockets on a United Nations Multidimensional Integrated Stabilization Mission in Mali's (MINUSMA) peacekeeping forces in northern Mali. The terrorist group Ansar Dine claimed responsibility for the attacks that resulted in the deaths of 3 and wounding 20 people. Ansar Dine is a militant Islamic group led by Iyad Ag Ghaly, one of the most prominent leaders of the Tuareg rebellion in the 1990s. Ansar Dine, was created on 2012 and still operating now, is a very active Islamic Terrorist Jihadist group. It wants the imposition of strict Sharia law across Mali.

December 2, 2015, U.S. - San Bernardino, California, was the scene of a terrorist Islamic attack by two Jihadists that attacked and killed many civilians attending a holiday event. Perpetrators Syed Farook and Tashfeen Malik left their six-month-old daughter with Farook's mother at their home the morning of the attack, saying they were going to doctor's appointment. The couple had other plans!!! He and his wife made sure to execute them. He was a health inspector for the San Fernardino County Department of Public Health, attending a departmental event at the banquet room of the inland Regional Center, with other employees. There was a total of 91 invited guests, with 75-80 people stated to have been in attendance. Coworkers reported that Farook had been quiet and left midway through the event. However, he had time to pose for photos with coworkers. They were armed with semi-automatic pistols and rifles, around 11am, opened fire on those in attendance. The entire shooting took no more than four minutes, firing between 65 and 75 bullets. The perpetrators departed the scene before police arrived. They killed 14 civilians and wounded 22 civilians, plus 2 police officers later. Farook was an American-born U.S. citizen of Pakistani descent, and his wife Malik was a Pakistani-born lawful permanent resident of the United States. After the shooting, the couple fled in a rented sport utility vehicle. Four hours later, police pursued their vehicle and killed them in a shootout. Sources reported that Malik pledged bay'ah (allegiance) to the leader of ISIL on a Facebook account associated with her as the attack was underway. The FBI revealed that the perpetrators were homegrown violent extremists inspired by foreign terrorist groups. They have become radicalized over several years prior to the attack, consuming "poison on the internet" and expressing a commitment to jihadism and martyrdom in private messages to each other. They had traveled to Saudi Arabia in the years before the attack. They collected a large amount of weapons in their home.

December 5, 2015, Chad- four female suicide bombers from the militant Islamist group Boko Haram attacked the Chadian island of Koulfoua on Lake Chad, killing at least 19 and injuring more than 130 people. Two of the blasts came out from the center of the market and a third in the street as people fled. Boko Haram tactics are to attack villages, get potential suicide bombers and fanatics from the population, train them, then use them as weapons or suicide soldiers. Boko Haram has also been known to kidnap girls, whom after an intense training, they use as militants. On April 2014, 276 female students were kidnapped from Government Secondary School in the town of Chibok in Borno State, Nigeria. The students have been forced to convert to Islam and into marriage with members of Boko Haram. Many of the students were taken to the neighboring countries of Chad and Cameroon, with sightings of the students by villagers living in the Sambisa Forest. The forest is considered a refuge for Boko Haram. December's four female suicide bombers rang a bell on how Boko Haram's plan is to extend their militants and fighters to women and children (later on). Shekau (Boko Haram's leader) claimed that "Allah instructed him to sell them (women) and that he will carry out his instructions". He also said, "Slavery is allowed in his religion, and he shall capture people and make them slaves". He said the girls should not have been in school and instead should have been married since girls as young as nine are suitable for marriage!!! Chibok is primarily a Christian village and Shekau acknowledged that many of the girls seized were not Muslims: he said "The girls that have not accepted Islam, they are now gathered in numbers... and we treat them well the way the Prophet Muhammad treated the infidels he seized." Barbaric and unhuman are two descriptions to what Boko Haram is doing.

December 6, 2015, Yemen- the governor of the southern port city of Aden in Yemen was killed in a car bomb which was carried out by ISIS. December 8, 2015, Afghanistan- a suicide attack was coordinated just hours after a "message to Obama", was posted on a video site by Taliban warning U.S. troops. The Taliban claimed responsibility for the suicide bombers who penetrated the security Kandahar Airfield, battling with Afghan soldiers for few hours. 50 civilians died, along 11 attackers, and 35 people were wounded. December 8, 2015, Egypt- an explosive device by Islamists targeting a military convoy went off in Rafah, killed four (4) Egyptian security personnel and injured other 4 people. December 9, 2015, Iraq- a suicide bomber detonated his explosives at the doorway of a Shiite mosque, resulting in the killing of more than 11 people and wounding more than 20 others. December 11, 2015, Afghanistan- Taliban militants detonated a car bomb and stormed a guesthouse near the Spanish embassy in the Shirpour district of Kabul. Nine (9) people died in the attack; four Afghans, two Spanish and including 3 perpetrators' Taliban fighters. December 11, 2015,

Syria- 60 people died and injuring more than 80 in the town of Tell Tamer, in three truck bombs by ISIS. December 12, 2015, Syria-Islamists detonated a car bomb near a hospital in central Homs, killed 16 and wounded more than 54 other people. Responsibility for the attack was taken by ISIS. The Jihadist Islamist militant blew himself up killing rescuers who were trying to save hospital attack victims. ISIS later claimed responsibility for the appalling attack which planned out the attack to take as many innocent lives as possible. The militant blew himself up in a crowd of people (brave men and women) who were desperately trying to save victims of a nearby hospital car bombing. The bomber parked his car and detonated the 150kg of explosives near the city's largest hospital. He then set off his suicide explosives belt as scores of people gathered at the scene to help the injured victims. December 12, 2015, Iraq- a militant detonated his explosives in a truck at an Iraqi position near the Saudi border, killed 6 and injured 14. December 13, 2015, Nigeria- Boko Haram Islamists, some using machetes, attacked residents of the villages of Warwara, Mangari, and Bura-Shika, resulting in the death of 30 and wounding more than 20. Most of the victims were slaughtered and some of the wounded had suffered machete cuts. The Islamists invaded the three villages, hacked and slaughtered their victims before they set the villages on fire. The latest deaths take the number of people killed in Nigeria since President Muhammadu Buhari took office in May to more than 1,530. Once he took office, he pledged to demolish Boko Haram. The few days coming proved him wrong, as two more attacks happened. December 21, 2015, Afghanistan- a suicide bomber on a motorbike killed six U.S. troops and wounded three in Kabul. December 26, 2015, Nigeria- Boko Haram again raiding houses and killing innocent civilians in northern Nigeria. The toll was of at least 14 people who died on this Christmas day gun attack. December 28, 2015, Afghanistan- a Taliban suicide bomber killed at least one (1) person and wounded more than 33 in an attack on a road near a school close to Kabul International Airport.

December 28, 2015, Nigeria- Boko Haram militants was responsible for the killing of 26 people and wounding another 85 in an attack perpetrated by fourteen Islamist female suicide bombers between the age of 12 and 18. They attempted to simultaneously attack the city of Maiduguri. Seven of the bombers were shot dead by Nigerian forces while three managed to escape and detonate themselves in Baderi general area and near a mosque. December 29, 2015, Pakistan- a Taliban suicide bomber detonated his explosives in front of a Pakistani government building. The blast killed 26 people and more than 50 were wounded. December 29, 2015, Russia- ISIS claimed the shooting in Derbent, Dagestan; southern Russia. Islamist gunmen opened fire on a group of local residents who were visiting a viewing platform at the Derbent citadel, a Unesco World Heritage site, killing one (1) and injuring 11 others. The al-Nusra Front, an al-Qaeda linked group active in Syria, has called on jihadists to organize attacks in Russia in retaliation for the country's bombing campaign in support of the Syrian government. Russia has been bombing IS and other groups it considers terrorists, some of which are backed by Western powers.

More than 210 Terrorist Islamic attacks had been registered for the period 2010 till 2015. From 2010 till end 2015, it has been more than 3,045 killed and more than 5,062 innocent victims injured in attacks related to Islamic jihadist.

Next terrorist attack.

From the first attack beginning 2010 till beginning January 2015, we have reached the number of 104, such terrorist Islamic attacks all over the world. Then, from beginning 2015 till end 2015, there were 106 tragic attacks. In one year, 2015, we had more Terrorist Islamic attacks than 5 years all together.

2016 will see less attacks in the west and more in the third world countries. Taliban Terrorist group have intensified their attacks in Afghanistan soil at the end of 2015 and beginning of 2016.

Al-Shabaab, Taliban, ISIS, Boko Haram will see their activities picking up pace at the year of 2016.

From 2017 and up, there will be a new sort of attacks; a new trend and generation more focused on occupying lands, and claiming properties and territories.

Islamist Terrorist attacks would never end, unless the religion is either abolished or modified. For that reason we won't be able to comment and present all the attacks the world survived. The attacks presented in this essay focused on a determined period; combining attacks occurred in the 20th century and beginning of 21st century, precisely end of 2015.

For the main reason related to the impossibility to keep on redacting and reporting everyday attacks on any "printed" book, we limited the count to the deadline by the end of the year 2015.

To be able to spot the next coming terrorist attack, it is primordial to know the past and history of each terrorist attack that occurred at least in the last 10 years. Islamic terrorist organizations and groups don't stop from hiring new people to do their dirty jobs.

They go through screening to determine who can do such attacks without fear or hesitation.

Some questions have to be presented to get to know what criteria they take into consideration when they look for Terrorists or potential individuals.

Who are they? Where they come from, age, race, origins, and backgrounds? All these information can determine the motives that push them to go with their terrorist attacks.

If any individual or any entire entity; FBI, CIA or any other intelligence or national security administration can break down the pattern that lead to Islamic Terrorist attacks, they can be prevented from happening. They are Terrorists, but also just human. They can make some mistakes and be caught. Knowing their next move has to be a priority for any government or state department to stop them. It takes only one day, one hour few minutes to stop those attacks from happening. Islamic Terrorist attacks need to be predictable. They are like Lotto Numbers, you only wish you knew those numbers the day before, and then you ask yourself, why we didn't know those terrorists intentions the day before the attack?

Safety and security can be the solution to stop Terrorist attack. But in most of the time, it is only a way to slow down their imminent presence. Prevention is huge task and cost lot of money. People can't be living in fear all their lives. Societies can't afford to babysit their citizens all the time. We should do better as humans, and stop the fight between races.

Securing the whole country is impossible. Preventing Terrorists attacks from happening is also impossible, but, security has to be push one step up to stop the bleeding.

The Terrorist attacks presented in this book have received a sufficient media coverage. However, other incidents related to Islamic assault could have occurred by individuals or groups, but either, they didn't get enough attention by public, or had not been classified as Islamic terrorist attacks, or the perpetrators had carefully hidden their identities and nobody heard of them. Therefore, many other attack could have been happened, but aren't treated here.

Those are lot of Jihadists acts. Too many to stop. The world is a big place to control such fanatics. We should be together in the fight. One strategy cannot be the solution for all those attacks. The way to stop those attacks should be articulated in a different way for each nation. A European nation won't be able to stop such a cancer, a terrorist problem in the same way as an American nation or South-American or African nation. An Islamic nation has a part of the blame for such extension of extremists, so to stop terrorists, for them, it should be easier. It should be different to control such spread.

How can we, once of all, stop this?

So, it was not frequently happening before the 80s or 70s. How can we go back to those days?

Is it because of the Israeli-Palestinian conflict? Is it because of a religious clash between Islam and Christianity? It is a combination of both.

What started as a local and more regional problem, became more of a global issue. The Palestinian-Israeli conflict has helped on fueling more and more hatred from one side to the other.

The Munich Olympic Massacre, September 5, 1972; eight Palestinian terrorists walked into the Olympic Village in Munich, West Germany, captured eleven Israeli athletes, and, after a failed rescue effort by German authorities, nine of the hostages massacred and five terrorists killed. It was a major turning point of how the world should have stand together to stop the spread of such Islamic terrorist problem. What have been done after that incident, was not smartly enough to banish the extension of an evil concept and idea (Islamic Jihad).

Because of the Israeli-Palestinian conflict and as a result to justify attacking them in Israel we end up in such a mess. Attacking the people of Jewish decedent in Israel was not enough. The main reason for that insufficiency is security. Israel has been building its state around security, and all aspects of life in Israel goes around safety as number one priority. All that area surrounding Israel, Lebanon, Syria or Egypt is considered a war zone, therefore, not too much importance is giving to killings or terrorizing humans there.

Two points made the Islamic jihadists move their operations to civilians all over the world: strong security in Israel, and the existence of a zone war in the area, which makes it, after a while, less mediate, therefore, less important. For example, bombing and killing one civilian in a western nation, such USA or France, has more influence than killing ten civilians in Lebanon or even Israel.

As a result, those terrorists chose to attack anybody related to the western concept in other countries to justify the need to such attacks, anywhere and anyway regardless of where they reside. USA and Europe by definition have been all an ally to Israel, so attacking Europe and USA was going to happen anyway, it was just a question of how, and only a matter of time.

To understand the concept of a next terrorist attack, it will be primordial to study every Islamic Terrorist Organization, and its motifs. It is also important to see the demography and ages of its population. For example, when Boko Haram abducted girls aged 14-15, probably nobody thought if they would be using them as fighters, and then they did use them late 2015 as they grow 16 or 17 years-old. The same concept would assume that by end 2016, most of those abducted girls would be pregnant so it would be hard for them to be fighters. On 2017, no more attacks by them could be suspected to be happening or reported if they have to take care of their kids. This reality would change the number of terrorist attacks perpetrated by Islamic Terrorist from Boko Haram terrorist group.

The same concept could apply to other terrorist groups operating under the umbrella of Islam. It might not include women and their need to be pregnant or caring for their kids, but it could be another detour's that would cause the suspension or extension of such Islamic terrorist attacks.

Another way to prevent or stop a terrorist attack is just to foil the attack. Tens of them attacks have been occurred then diverted from happening, because of the courage of some or the diligence of the force of authorities. In 2001, an example of how a plot can be foiled is of Richard Reid, aka "Shoe Bomber", onboard Flight 63 Paris to Miami, attempted to ignite explosives in his shoe. One of the latest examples is of the German police that arrested, on February 4, 2016, four Algerian citizens, who were planning major Islamic State ISIS attack in Berlin. The police arrested them of links to the IS group after raids targeting several sites, including refugee shelters where some the suspects lived.

Every year, there are many plots stopped in relation of prospective Islamic Attacks. Those thwarted Islamic terrorist attacks should be met with an iron fist response. And the future attackers should get a rigorous consequence of their fail attempt with a jail time no less than 30 years.

Leadership profile.

After years and years of fighting, the conflict became more religious than just a Palestine-Israeli conflict. And that's where it turned out to be more complicated. It changed to a clash of cultures, of color and race, and of course religion.

Governments, political parties and leaders have also been using it to get more power and political influence. Yasser Arafat, ex-Palestinian President is a good example of how a Head of a State could be a Terrorist. Before he died, the world started to realize how he fueled all the terrorist groups to kill innocent people in Israel or other parts of the worlds. He used his power to organize many acts of Terrorism against innocent people. Another example is of the Moroccan royal family. During decades, they have been promoting terror within their own subjects. All Moroccan kings during centuries have been using the religion of Islam to consolidate their political power within and outside of the country.

Such conflict of interests have created Terrorists groups, and their leaders have become more and more influencing in the power decision-taken. Most of the Terrorist groups' leaders are military-trained individuals that have connections with the political power. They seek mostly a recognition and in some cases independency from the main power governing the country. They need money and arms to succeed in their quest to the top of the political chain. Their main tactic is using religion for the sole purpose of accomplishing their goals.

To understand the reasons related to any attack, it is important to study the people responsible for such attacks. What motivate them is the main question to be studied.

First question most of the counter-terrorism departments and intelligence agencies present themselves with is to know who did such attacks and how to stop them from going forward with these attacks.

Studying the terrorists and their origins, backgrounds, families, race, schools they went to, childhood, friends… is very important to know their motives. But such materials can never be enough in order to catch other terrorists. Those materials are needed to report suspicious behaviors from other suspected terrorists or radical groups. Those factors have nothing to do, or little to do with their motives. Most, if not all of the Terrorists are Muslims. Religion can be the one and only related link between most of the terrorist attackers.

One of the most radical Islamic Terrorist leader was Usama Ben Laden. All other Islamist Terrorist leaders of Islamic Terrorist groups see on Ben Laden a model to follow. They grew up in an era where hitting and killing other "infidels" are seen as a pride to their actions. Leaders with more savage thoughts than their predecessors. It explain the barbaric actions Boko Haram Terrorist group handle their terror actions. Another example is of ISIS. Both their militias have no fear or humanity in the way they execute their victims. It is a tactic taught by their leaders.

To end Islamic Terrorist attacks, it is primordial to get rid of their leaders. It is a priority to abolish who they see as a role model. People rely on them, they see them as a way to get a rewarding future in their society. Most of the militants try to escalate to the same level where their leaders operate. They consider themselves soldiers for a one cause; which is to execute any orders giving to them by their leaders. Every terrorist act committed by Muslim militants, groups or individuals are professed by Islamic or Islamist motivations or goals set by such leaders.

Islamic Terrorist groups operate and rely on particular interpretations of the tenets of the Quran and the Hadith, which are also translated by the leaders of such groups. They cite the scriptures and justify violent methods including mass murder, genocide, child molestation and slavery. Leaders of those Islamic terror groups have the main job of propaganda with the values of Islam, and promoting a hostile environment to their benefits. An environment where anybody who doesn't respond to the needs and necessity of the group should be annihilated. They also establish a code of conduction relying on the Prophet Mahomet's way of life. Such code is basically a copy of how people used to live back then in the Prophet's time. According to them, the whole world should be Islamize and women and children degraded to slavery. As a result to reward their followers, the leaders always make sure two message should be understood, which are: death is the only logical consequence for "infidels" (anybody who doesn't believe in Allah or doesn't apply by the exact word everything Islam dictate), and promising an eternal life (after death) to whoever go and plan to commit a terrorist (suicide) violent act against those infidel people.

Leaders of such Terrorist Islamic groups have become more and more radicals. In recent decades, incidents of Islamic terrorism have occurred on a global scale, occurring not only in Muslim-majority countries, but also abroad in Europe, the United States and Asia, and such attacks have targeted Muslims and non-Muslims.

There about more than 30 Islamic Terrorists known groups operating in the world. The most famous ones are known to be Al-Qaeda, ISIS, Taliban, Boko Haram, Hamas, Hezbollah, Abu Sayyaf and Al-Gama'a al-Islamiyya. Each of these groups have other affiliate groups coordinated between them. Operations can range from killing people or just stealing properties. If Al-Qaeda is a worldwide organization with not only one country to belong to, other groups can be limited to some areas, like Palestinian Islamic

Jihad operating mostly in Gaza Strip and West Bank. Here is the list of all the Islamic Terrorist groups:

Abu Sayyaf, Philippines.

Al-Aqsa Martyrs' Brigades, Gaza Strip and West Bank.

Al-Gama'a al'Islamiyya, Egypt.

Al-Qaeda, worldwide.

A-Shabaab, Somalia.

Ansar al-Islam, Iraq.

Ansar al-Sharia, Libya.

Armed Islamic Group (GIA), Algeria.

Boko Haram, Nigeria.

Caucusus Emirate (IK), Russia.

East Turkestan Islamic Movement (ETIM), China.

Egyptian Islamic Jihad, Egypt.

Great Eastern Islamic Raiders' Front (IBDA-C), Turkey.

Hamas, Gaza Strip and West Bank.

Harkat-ul-Mujahideen al-Alami, Pakistan.

Hezbollah, Lebanon.

Islamic Movement of Central Asia, Central Asia.

Islamic Movement of Uzbekistan, Uzbekistan.

Islamic State of Iraq and the Levant (ISIS), worldwide.

Jaish-e-Mohammed, Pakistan and Kashmir.

Jamaat Ansar al-Sunna, Iraq.

Jemaah Islamiyah, Indonesia.

Lashkar-e-Taiba, Pakistan and Kashmir.

Lashkar-e-Jhangvi, Pakistan.

Moro Islamic Liberation Front, Philippines.

Moroccan Islamic Combatant Group, Morocco and Europe.

Palestinian Islamic Jihad, Gaza Strip and West Bank.

Tawhid and Jihad, Iraq.

All the Islamic groups are not limited geographically to one area and can operate, depending on their financial capabilities anywhere.

End of terrorism.

Managing time and space is the key to stop terrorism.

What did the terrorists gain from all the attacks they perpetrated? The only thing they get is the coverage by the media. What was their goal, purpose? Hey terrorist, you can't possibly think you could kill the whole world. Hey Terrorist, wake up from the dream, there is no heaven waiting for you after death. Hey Terrorist, we understand your motives, they don't make sense, but its ok we understand them. Hey terrorist, you are making it even worse for your co-Muslim people to live and be liked. Hey terrorist, go do something better with your time than just planning on killing others, you are a coward.

Understanding terrorists, or for instance a fanatic Muslim's mind; or the way they think would be the correct way to stop them from killing innocent people. Those terrorists are humans too, therefore, they must feel the benefits of love or peace. How did they end up to be such evils? Arabs, for instance, 600 years ago were so much better humans than the Arabs nowadays. Why? Back then, they were more civilized than now?

Why the terrorist attacks have been in a fluctuation patterns from up to down or up to down? From beginning 2010 till end of 2014, 5 years have seen 104 Islamic Terrorist attacks, and only one year after, 2015, just in one it has seen more attacks, 106 attacks from January till December of 2015. Also 6 attacks in 2007, 7 attacks in 2008 and just 4 attacks in 2009, should be justified by other factors that push the Islamic Terrorist to either intensifies their attacks or minimize them. A low number in the end of 2008 or rise of attacks in 2015 could be explained by various factors. It was few attacks between 2007 and 2009, no more than 20. Is it because of the election of Obama, people in the Middle East, Muslims and Arabs felt accepted by such president, so they lower their attacks volume in the western countries and all over the world? Or is it because of the economic crash, so Terrorist were just satisfied for the way things are going wrong in the western countries that they didn't have to worry about killings its people? So basically the bad economy is doing just a fine job to punish the capitalism, a concept Islamic Jihadist hates. The death of Osama Bin Laden was a stimulus for more attacks? The Arab spring; all the revolts against the tyrants, presidents, governments and Kings in the Arab worlds, did it create more hatred toward the western's way of life? Is it because there was no concrete results after all the manifestations, riots that had been carried out by people for months, years? Will that explain the attacks that have been intensified after the stagnancy of such countries who went through the "Arab Spring", because their economy and lifestyle have been stagnant, undeveloped, poor and bad? Arab Spring started on 2011, it refers to the democratic uprisings that arose independently and spread across the Arab word in 2011. The movement originated in Tunisia December 2010 and quickly took hold in Egypt, Libya, Syria, Bahrain, Saudi Arabia, and Jordan. Would that explain the rise of attacks we survived during 2015? After years of fighting, no real improvements in the Arab world would lead to anger toward western countries? It was the start of the fanatic Islamic Terrorist that have spread all over the planet. Those Jihadist militants were asking for more power after most of the Dictators, Presidents and even kings lost most of their power and in some cases all of it. Citizens in countries like Tunisia, Egypt, Libya, Yemen, Nigeria, Syria, Iraq, and even Morocco, have developed a certain sympathy to Islamic uprising ideas. These ideas are poison to the development of any civilization, and Islam should be changing the concept to how its followers see the rest of the world.

www.ingramcontent.com/pod-product-compliance
Lightning Source LLC
Chambersburg PA
CBHW072049280526

45788CB00006B/2239